又见情人节

温迪·蔻普诗选

[英]温迪·蔻普 著 徐艳萍 译

陕西师范大学出版总社

图书代号：WX18N1739

Copyright © 2019 by Wendy Cope
图书版权登记号：25-2019-051

图书在版编目（CIP）数据

又见情人节：温迪·蔻普诗选：英汉对照/（英）温迪·蔻普著；徐艳萍译. — 西安：陕西师范大学出版总社有限公司，2019.4
ISBN 978-7-5695-0474-3

Ⅰ.①又… Ⅱ.①温… ②徐… Ⅲ.①英语—汉语—对照读物 ②诗集—英国—现代 Ⅳ.①H319.4：I

中国版本图书馆CIP数据核字（2018）第290331号

又见情人节：温迪·蔻普诗选
YOU JIAN QINGRENJIE:WENDY COPE SHIXUAN

[英]温迪·蔻普 著　徐艳萍 译

出 版 人	刘东风
责任编辑	王奉文
责任校对	陈君明
封面设计	@xuxue_design
出版发行	陕西师范大学出版总社
	（西安市长安南路199号，邮编710062）
网　　址	http://www.snupg.com
印　　刷	山东临沂新华印刷物流集团有限责任公司
开　　本	880mm×1230mm　1/32
印　　张	7.5
插　　页	4
字　　数	110千
版　　次	2019年4月第1版
印　　次	2019年4月第1次印刷
书　　号	ISBN 978-7-5695-0474-3
定　　价	38.80元

读者购书、书店添货或发现印装质量问题，请与本公司营销部联系、调换。
电话：（029）85307864　85303629　传真：（029）85303879

诗人温迪和她的诗歌风格

一

温迪·寇普（Wendy Cope，1945—）是一位颇受欢迎的英国当代女诗人，被《每日电讯报》称为"诗坛奇才"，《伦敦书评》称她为"喷气机时代的丁尼生"。她的诗以语言直白简洁、睿智诙谐和韵律完美而著称。前坎特伯雷大主教罗恩·威廉姆斯（Rowan Williams，1950—）是她的粉丝，称其为英国当代最睿智幽默的诗人。2010年，她被英女王授予大英帝国勋章（OBE），荣获勋爵称号。

温迪1945年7月21日生于英格兰肯特郡的埃里斯。她的父亲起步于一家电子公司的制图学徒，继而成为制图员，最后成为埃里斯Mitchells百货商店的经理。她的妈妈是爸爸的下属（后成为其秘书）。五十五岁的经理因丧偶成了鳏夫（第一次婚姻没有孩子），二十八岁的秘书嫁给了"钻石王老五"（当时还有好几位单身女士梦想成为经理的新夫人）。

温迪的母亲自幼失怙，孤儿寡母（母亲和外祖母）相依为命，生活很是艰难。温迪母亲成为埃里斯Mitchells百货商店的雇员后，母女俩的命运才得以改变。

鳏夫经理向未婚女秘书求婚，颇有自知之明的他坦言："当然，我有点老了。"

小经理近三十岁的秘书机警地答道："不，你不老。你就像彼得·潘（同名小说《彼得·潘》中一个永远长不大的孩子）一样，永远不会老。"

婚后，两人借用小说中人物的名字，妻子称丈夫"彼得"，丈夫叫妻子"温迪"。"钻石王老五"给喜欢音乐的少妻购买了钢琴。经理秘书经过华丽转身，不仅过上了衣食无忧的优越生活，还成了精明、能干的女商人——百货商店的真正主管，并且在公共事务中身兼数职。诗人温迪的外祖母在温迪母亲结婚后一直跟着女儿住，打理家务。经理夫人迎来了人生的辉煌时期，期间，两次与另一个嫁给老夫的少妻——撒切尔夫人碰面。

诗人"温迪"的名字源于母亲身怀六甲时，在黑斯廷斯市（Hastings）邂逅了一艘写着温迪·玛丽的小船，"温迪"就成了即将出生的小宝宝的名字，夫妇俩坚信他们未来的孩子是个女孩。

温迪很早就上学了，她上的第一所学校是修道院学校。在那里，当一位修女给她们讲童贞女玛丽亚时，幼稚、单纯的温迪举手问了个让老师很尴尬的问题：

"Miss，什么是童贞女？"

"童贞女就是一个从不做错事的年轻女子。"

"什么错事也没做过？从不犯错？即使她是小姑娘的时候也不犯错？"

"是的。从不犯错。"

几年后，温迪才知道了童贞女的真正含义。

温迪喜欢外祖母胜过自己的父母。外祖母教幼小的温迪字母、音标和单词。识字后的温迪就喜欢上了阅读，有了"书虫"的雅号。许是日渐衰老的父亲喜欢清静的缘故，他不大喜欢小孩子在身边，七岁的温迪就被送到了寄宿学校（外祖母没有话语权）。过早离开父母过集体生活的她也早早地不再依恋父母。成年后的她记述了当年在查令十字街火车站挥别父母的情形：

在学校列车停靠的站台上
七岁的她没有哭
就像她在书中读到的小女生
她笑着，聊着
她吻别了父母，然后离开
她从此再也没有真正地回来

温迪坦诚和父母的关系不好。成为诗人的她年少时曾对母亲说"我恨你"，她说，那时她是当真的。也许这与她很小就被父母送去寄宿有关。

不容争辩这是否是真的
她很爱你，她是这么对你说的
只有她知道什么对你最好
让她来告诉你该做什么，该去哪里

她很爱你，她是这么对你说的
这就是为何要把你送到寄宿学校去
让她来告诉你该做什么，该去哪里
不要违背她的旨意

…………
让妈妈难过，就是你的错

　　幼小的温迪是一个坚强的女孩，她没有因为要去寄宿学校而哭闹。学校里的欺辱现象时有发生，只是她不参与这种欺辱行动。

我们是女汉子，没有爸妈的照顾
我们也活了过来

…………

私下里我也脆弱
担心被取乐

"取乐"就是我们说的欺辱
受辱者由飞扬跋扈的大姐大选出

…………

时而一声大喊：
"追特鲁迪·蒂普尔！"

…………

我没有参与。当然
并不是因为我跑不动

因为温迪不擅长游戏比赛,小学教育并没有给她留下温馨的记忆。

当他们在户外组队做游戏时
站在栅栏边的她和我
总是被挑剩下的两个
…………
十一岁时,我俩上了不同的学校
我终于能以牙还牙
把会打曲棍球而不会拼写的他们嘲笑

小米勒却死了,那年她刚十二岁

博览群书的温迪中学毕业后到牛津大学圣希尔达学院主修历史,这是因为她的中学英语老师对她父母说她没有学术天赋,不适合上大学,而她的中学历史老师对她评价甚高。在温迪看来,她在牛津大学的学习经历是"彻头彻尾的失败"。在校期间的她很不快活,人生中第一次也是唯一一次有了自杀的念头。甚至在工作后的几年里,她一直不愿走进牛津这座城市。

从牛津大学毕业的温迪在牛津的威斯敏斯特教育学院接受了教师职业培训,后在伦敦的一所小学执教。她负责四年级的一个"乱班",她的教学工作涉及给孩子们读诗,教孩子们欣赏诗,鼓励孩子们写诗。她自己也开始写诗,并发现了自己的文学创造力,应了这句名言"天生我材必有用"。

温迪四十岁时,外祖母去世。温迪把外祖母的一生浓缩为《名字》一诗(见本书)。

温迪年少时受母亲的熏陶,学会了弹钢琴,后来在大学,又自学了吉他。成为一名小学教师后，她的音乐特长有了用武之地。她后来成了这所小学的音乐教师。1984年起，温迪一边任学校的兼职音乐教师，一边当专栏作家。

温迪1986年出版的第一部诗集《给金斯利·艾米斯冲可可饮料》(*Making Cocoa for Kingsley Amis*)引起了极大的反响，诗集进入了畅销书榜单，她一夜成名。该诗集使她荣获诗歌图书协会推荐奖（Poetry Book Society Recommendation）和乔姆利诗歌奖（Cholmondeley Award, 1987）。该诗集至今销售已近二十万册。她随后又出版了多部诗集，其中多部作品入选英国畅销书榜单。之后，她辞去教职，成了一名自由撰稿人，先后担任伦敦一教育权威杂志的艺术、评论编辑和杂志《观察家》的电视评论员等。

她1992年出版的《关切》(*Serious Concerns*)使她声誉更隆。此外，她还出版编辑了数本诗歌选集，诸如，《那是新月吗？》(*Is That The New Moon?* 1989)、《理查德诙谐诗集》(*The Orchard Book of Funny Poems*, 1993)、《菲波床头故事集》(*The Faber Book of Bedtime Stories*, 1999)、《地球上的天堂：101首快乐诗歌》(*Heaven on Earth: 101 Happy Poems*)、《搞笑的一面：101首幽默诗》(*The Funny Side: 101 Humorous Poems*)，和两本儿童诗集《动动你的大拇指》(*Twiddling Your Thumbs*, 1988)、《河的女儿》(*The River Girl*, 1991)等等。她为儿童创作的诗歌也广泛地被编录入集。1995年，温迪荣获美国文学和艺术学院迈克尔·布劳德谐趣诗奖。1998年，她被英国BBC电台听众推荐为继泰德·休斯之后的英国桂冠诗人（后安德鲁·莫伸获选）。2001年，诗集《如果我不知道》(*If I Don't Know*)荣获诗歌图书协会推荐奖和乔姆利诗歌奖。2009年，当安德鲁·莫伸桂冠诗人的头衔到期时，她被认为是获选可能性最大的候选人（后卡洛·安·达菲当选）。2010年，她被英女王授予OBE(大英帝国勋章)，荣获勋爵称号。她的诗歌被灌录成诗歌档案。她本人多次受邀到欧美其他国家朗诵其诗歌作品，讲授诗歌创作。继2011年出版的诗集《家庭价值观》（*Family Values*），2018年3月，温迪又推出新诗集《轶事证据》（*Anecdote Evidence*）。英国国家图书馆购买收藏了她的档案文件（手稿、笔记、四万封电子邮件及学校报告等），这是迄今为止英国国家图书馆收购电子邮件最多的一次。

温迪四十八岁时和现在的丈夫拉克伦·麦金农（Lachlan Mackinnon）携手（确立了同居关系）。拉克伦也是一位诗人，比温迪小十一岁，毕业于牛津大学。拉克伦执教于温彻斯特公学，1994年，温迪随他前往温彻斯特。拉克伦2011年获乔姆利诗歌奖。2013年，两位诗人携手度过了美好的十九年后，在拉克伦的恳请下，两人步入婚姻殿堂。成为"丈夫"和"妻子"后的他们感受到了同居关系下感受不到的美满幸福。为了能和妻子一起住在伊利过自己想过的生活，拉克伦提前从温彻斯特公学退休。

二

温迪被前坎特伯雷大主教罗恩·威廉姆斯称为英国当代最睿智幽默的诗人。她的诗歌语言直白简洁、睿智诙谐，韵律完美，颇具魅力。不仅在英语世界广受赞誉，还受到世界各地读者的喜爱。

1. 动人心弦的永恒主题

温迪的诗歌没有鼓吹或宣扬崇高抑或博大的思想，她更多地关注着平常人的平常生活及对平凡生活的感受，除了对现实生活及男性世界的不足大胆地表达自己的见解、嘲讽之外,她的诗歌更多地表述男女之爱、孩子之爱、生活之爱等。她的诗歌以"情"动人,她独到细腻的描述往往能让读者产生强烈的情感共鸣,特别是以女性的爱恨情仇为主题的诗歌。她的诗歌惟妙惟肖地描述了在"爱"的不同境遇下的女性内心纷繁复杂的感受,诸如期盼、焦虑、失落、绝望甚至痛恨等。她细腻的笔墨真实地刻画了她对生活以及对女性的认知,从坠入爱河的心境、享受爱情的心情、对生活的热爱到失恋的沮丧和对不如意生活的逆反心理等,包罗万象。读她的诗,读者仿佛突然意识到自己昔日或者当下的烦忧并非个人的不幸,而是许多人都曾经历的苦难。

如果说她的《午饭后》(*After the Lunch*)描述的是一位情感内敛的女子不经意间坠入爱河的那份欲罢不能的炽热情愫,那么《走火入魔》(*Going Too Far*)则描述了一位视爱如生命的女子的痴情和怨恚。

当我发现你的名字在新的电话簿里
我就把电话簿搂在怀里
真是走火入魔

无论你在哪里,我敢打赌
你都不会把电话簿搂在怀里

诗歌《口信儿》(*Message*)同样淋漓尽致地刻画了一个坠入情网而又不敢造次的女子的内心世界,她独特的描述让人为之动容:

我知道你喜欢我,但我

不敢再给你打电话。我只有竭力地
通过伦敦的空气向你发送我思念的波
倘若你收到了,切莫犹豫——
请立刻抓起电话,拨我的号码

爱情这一奇妙的混合体可谓甜蜜的痛苦——使人欢喜,也使人烦忧。爱情并非都一帆风顺,一波三折的爱情跋涉让人沮丧,甚至绝望。她的诗歌《痛失男友》描述了这种挫败、颓唐,甚至发狂的心境:

他搬出的那天真是糟透了
那个晚上她像跌进地狱一般
他的空缺并非无法对付
但开瓶器怎么也找不见

独特的感受才能成就好的诗篇。热烈、痴狂是爱,平平淡淡又何尝不是?相爱的人都知道,只要在一起,就是一种幸福。温迪借自己虚拟出的诗人斯特拉格内尔之笔写下这样的诗行:

树下,与一袋薯片在一起
还有一罐啤酒 一台收音机
和半睡半醒的你在布罗克韦尔公园
布罗克韦尔公园就仿佛天堂一般

这看似一个平淡的生活场景,通过温迪细腻的笔,寥寥几句就非同凡响。其中滋味只有深深爱过的人们才能体会。难怪有读者购买温迪的诗集在情人节作为礼物送给爱人。正如某文人评价的那样，在写关于爱情和男人的主题时，没有人可以胜过温迪。

2. 令人耳目一新的比喻

诗歌优于其他文体在于"诗歌是最佳词汇的最佳排列"（柯勒律治语）——有限的字数承载着无限的意义。诗人往往是语言大师，修辞高手。正如美国诗人罗伯特·弗罗斯特所言：诗歌就是用不同的方式表述常见的场景。温迪就是这方面的圣手。她的诗没有旁征博引，没有引经据典，只是用纯朴的语句将日常生活中的人或事娓娓道来，通俗易懂，既不晦涩，也不佯装高深莫测。温迪用朴实无华的语言结合巧妙绝伦、独特新奇的比喻，给我们司空见惯的东西赋予了新的意义和色彩。生活中屡见不鲜的场景通过她形象、巧妙的比喻给读者别开洞天的感觉，令人深思，使人忍俊不禁，甚至让人拍案叫绝。也许，这就是温迪的诗集一再进入畅销书榜单的原因。她也被称为"文学艺术家"。

太阳曾被莎士比亚比作"天堂之眼"，被哈代誉为"白昼之眼"，被叶赛宁比作"金盘"，而温迪貌似平淡却又新颖地写道：

挂在天边的太阳
此时就像举在水果盘上的一个橘子

以及：

东边发亮的足球
照得塔尔斯山一片光明

对每一个嗜酒的人，白酒都有种异样的亲切，而温迪的比喻更是惊人：

> 上等白酒
> 一定辛辣　醇香　清凉
> 宛如冬日鸟鸣

失恋的滋味大家都心知肚明，但在温迪笔下，其独特的比喻让这种失魂落魄的感觉不同凡响：

> 你从我身边跑开就像一个短跑运动员
> 而我爱你爱了近乎半年
> 世界成了一个冰箱　没了阳光

闹钟作为一件生活用品，是我们司空见惯的，但温迪赋予了它新的形象：

> 闹钟
> 仿佛一只困在大盒子里的昆虫
> 已感到惶恐

对于我们文明世界里的功臣——环卫工人，温迪给予他们和他们的工作极高的评价和尊重，"他看护着一排圣洗池般神圣的马桶"，这颠覆性的比喻令人对环卫工人和他们的恪尽职守肃然起敬。对于他们艰辛的工作，她无不同情："瘫坐在椅子上的他，像个S/一个渴望伸展为减号的S"，他们手中的拖把在她富有想象力的笔下成了"美杜莎那爬满毒蛇的头"。

每天，我们经历着日升日落，天亮天黑周而复始的生活，但

只有温迪,用她独特巧妙的比喻把昼夜轮回的自然现象描述得让人心悦诚服:

我们相伴的岁月犹如夜幕降临时的白昼
转瞬即逝

有的让人忍俊不禁:

早早醒了
听
鸟鸣
看
窗帘
恰似浸在奥妙洗涤剂里的衬衫
白了

温迪简洁、机智、诙谐的语言让人过目难忘,正如《诗歌评论》所说,温迪超乎寻常的机警和敏锐使她拥有了大批读者。

爱,千百年来文学艺术中的永恒主题,怎样海枯石烂的山盟海誓对读者来说似乎都很平淡,而温迪,没有引经据典,没有天荒地老的承诺,只淡淡地说了句:

我喜欢你胜过
想抽一支烟

经典诗源于亲身的感受。温迪曾经是个烟民,十七岁的温迪,一天吸二十支烟;近四十岁时,她吸烟的数量已升至一天三十支。后来的二十二年里,她没有一天中断过吸烟。用她的话说:"人们只是厌恶吸烟者,说吸烟影响健康,影响环境,可是能否理解一下对尼古丁上瘾的人,如果不被允许吸烟,他们就不能有效地工作。"嗜烟者想抽烟时的那种迫切的感觉恐怕不只温迪知道,但把这种感觉用来描写爱情,只有温迪想到了。

我们都熟知阳光,熟知穿过树梢的阳光会留下斑驳的影子,温迪在《一张老相片》(*On Finding an Old Photograph*)则这样写道:

穿过树梢的阳光
在他漂亮的袋子上打着补丁

我们周遭的世界在温迪的笔下变得妙不可言。塞缪尔·约翰逊说:"写作的唯一目的是让读者更好地享受生活或更顽强地忍受生活。"温迪就是这样借助修辞,借助自己丰富的想象和创造力使看似平淡的生活骤然生辉。通过她生花的妙笔,我们在平淡、平凡里看到了神奇,从而更加珍视生活中每一幕、每一景。

美国诗人爱伦·坡认为诗歌不宜过长,应该让读者能够一口气读完。作为修辞高手,温迪的诗歌大多短小精悍,语言简洁。她曾调侃道:"如果你不想让电视人用你的诗歌做傻事,就把诗歌写短些。"

3.睿智的幽默

常言道,幽默和风趣是智慧的闪现。温迪的诗以幽默和睿智著称。她的诗集《关切》(*Serious Concerns*,1992)和《如果我不知道》(*If I Don't Know*,2001)奠定了她英国杰出幽默诗人的地位。她的诗不仅使人发笑,还令人深思。貌似浅显、平淡的诗句幽默地道出了我们司空见惯的现象中的真谛并赋予它新的意义。

众所周知,对于没戴眼镜的近视者,眼前的世界自然模糊不清,没戴眼镜的温迪从卧室的后窗眺看,写下了这样诙谐的诗行:

那新绽放的奇异的柠檬黄的花
是什么花啊?
哦,是个足球

诗歌在当今世界鲜有读者,英国桂冠诗人安德鲁·莫伸曾写道:"当下,倘若有人看见你在火车上读诗,车厢顷刻间会空空如也。"诗人温迪深有同感,她说:"当今社会,和其他创作形式相比,人们不大接纳诗歌,不愿意费神去欣赏诗歌,至少对现代诗歌感兴趣的不多。"她以幽默诙谐,甚至夸张的口吻写道:

的确。我经常乘坐英伦地铁
东游西逛。我常说
如果你没有一张一等座车票
那你真的需要有一本诗集
如果你发现座位都已被占满
那就举起你的爱德华·托马斯、叶芝或庞德的诗集
车厢里被剧烈摇晃的其他乘客
就想远离你
对铁路社会学的最新研究显示
最好的办法是大声诵读:
读莫伸新诗集里的片言只语

你会立刻成一朵孤独的云
这是上天赐给隐士的良策
以证明诗歌的用途

美国诗人罗伯特·弗罗斯特曾说,所谓的诗歌,就是把普通的场景用不普通的方法表述出来。温迪以自己的睿智和幽默概述了诗歌当下艰难、尴尬的处境。完美巧妙地完成了美国诗人艾米莉·狄更生讲到的诗人肩上的重任——"讲真理,但要讲得含蓄。"当一档电视节目谈及诗歌的作用时,诗人温迪不无幽默地列举了诗歌的装饰(装饰碗碟、地铁站、铺路石)、盈利(通过评论诗歌、讲授诗歌、背诵诗歌等赚钱)和娱乐作用,她还引用彼得·伯特的话说"倘若没有了诗歌,别的不好的东西就会取代它"。

在中国,人们私下里把对性观念比较开放的女性讥讽为"公共汽车",诗人温迪独树一帜地说"该死的男人就像那该死的公共汽车":

该死的男人就像那该死的公共汽车
你在站牌下等了近乎一年
但当有一辆驶来时
其他两三辆也一同出现
看着公交车牌号忽闪忽闪
等你搭乘
仓促地浏览车身上的站名
没有太多时间定夺

一旦上错车,车不会倒回

跳下车，你只有立在半道儿眼巴巴地看着
小轿车、出租车和大货车从你身边飞驰而过
飞驰而过的还有时光和岁月

  相信这首充满怨艾但不乏真实、幽默的诗令读者，特别是女性读者无限感慨：一旦上错车（嫁错郎），只有下车，被甩在半路的你，此时只能眼睁睁看着"小轿车、出租车和大货车从你身边飞驰而过/飞驰而过的还有时光和岁月"。这就是温迪，只有她才能凭借自己的睿智、幽默和对生活深刻的洞察，以她精妙的比喻创造出这样的效果。正如《星期日电讯报》评论道：诗人温迪有颗细腻的心，她诗歌的伟大之处在于真。温迪承认自己是女权主义者，她认为向男性角色、男性社会挑战也无甚不妥。

  温迪坦承自己是一位具有幽默感的诗人。她说，事实上，她见到的诗人都具有幽默感，只是有些诗人没有把幽默感带入诗歌中。她甚至说："幽默常常源于悲惨和绝望，因为现实生活太糟糕了，我们只能付诸一笑。""为了让世界变得更好，我们必须要适度地高兴和乐观。"

  温迪从日常生活、工作中选取素材，凭借她的敏感、细腻，对一些僵硬甚至不可理喻的文字排版规则和规定，写下讥讽而不乏幽默的诗行：

体例混乱
艾米莉
喜欢用破折号
替代句号

当下，倘若

评论家和编辑

见到这癖好

他们会报警

寥寥几笔,对现实生活的不足和缺陷表达了她貌似诙谐实则严肃的见解。正如她的粉丝前坎特伯雷大主教罗恩·威廉姆斯所说,"温迪无疑是当代英国诗人中最睿智的一位,她道出了许多严肃的事实"。

4.完美的韵律

温迪不仅是修辞高手,更是韵律高手。她的诗歌基本都押韵。读者喜欢温迪的诗歌除了因其简洁的语言表达了别人无法表达的生活现实和社会现实之外,还因其诗歌富有完美的韵律。让诗行押韵对温迪来说似乎是小菜一碟,她顺手拈来的诗行就颇富韵味。

I worry about you-
So long since we **spoke**.
Love, are you downhearted,
Dispirited, **broke**?
I worry about you.
I can't sleep at ***night***[①].
Are you sad? Are you lonely?
Or are you all ***right***?
They say that men suffer,
As badly as **long**.

---

① 为了突显押韵的词,而又区别于上、下的韵脚,此处用斜体。下同——译注

I worry, I worry,

In case they are **wrong**.

以上这首《担心》（*Worry*）的结尾让人忍俊不禁。诗歌简单明了，因偶数行的押韵[əʊk]（spoke/broke），[aɪt] (night/right)，[ɒŋ]（long/wrong)显得极富韵味。

这首《即将离开》（*Leaving*）则是abab式的韵律：

Next summer? The summer **after**?
With luck we've a few more **years**
Of sunshine and drinking and **laughter**
And airports and goodbyes and **tears**.

第二个夏天？之后的又一个夏天？
真幸运，我们又多活了几年
享受着充满阳光、酒水和欢笑的生活
还有机场的挥别与泪眼婆娑

该诗寥寥数语抒发诗人对死亡表现的一种淡泊、平静——顺其自然；对生命、生活的感悟、感激。原文中第一、三行的韵脚['ɑːftə]（after/laughter）与第二、四行[ɪəs]（years/tears）的完美韵脚给诗歌增色不少。

温迪喜欢传统韵律规则，仿佛是喜欢穿着高跟鞋或冰刀跳舞的舞者，她创作了不少传统格律的四行诗、十四行诗、八行两韵诗。但温迪是旧瓶子装新酒，在传统诗歌格律的框架下用简洁诙谐的语言，运用巧妙的比喻，抒写对现代社会、现代生活和现代人的感悟。温迪的诗有着传统韵律诗的音律美，却没有传统韵律诗的晦涩。韵律（足踏冰刀或高跟鞋）的羁绊不仅没有让她的诗行失色，反而衬托出她是一个技艺高超的真正的诗人（舞者）。比如，这首受莎士比亚十四行诗（22）的启发而创作的五步阴阳格的十四行诗：

> My glass can't quite persuade me I am **old**—
> In that respect my ageing eyes are kind—
> But when I see a photograph, I'm **told**
> The dismal truth: I've left my youth behind.
> And when I try to get up from a **chair**
> My knees remind me they are past their best.
> The burden they have carried **everywhere**
> Is heavier now. No wonder they protest.
> Arthritic fingers, problematic **neck**,
> Sometimes causing mild to moderate pain,
> Could well persuade me I'm an ancient **wreck**
> But here's what helps me to feel young again:
>   My love, who fell for me so long ago,
>   Still loves me just as much, and tells me so.

该诗遵循着莎式十四行诗的传统韵律abab cdcd efef gg，但用词简单易懂，讲述现代人对现实生活的感悟——年华老去。第一、二行是典型的温迪式的幽默：

> My glass can't quite persuade me I am old—
> In that respect my ageing eyes are kind—

> 镜子并未使我意识到我容颜已老
> 这么说来,我的老花眼还挺仁慈的

接着是历数细枝末节来证明年华已逝,但在第三节往第四节过渡时,语气陡转,告慰我们,虽然我们无法把握住自己的青春年华,但我们可以把持住爱。完美的韵脚[əʊ](ago/so)与意味深长的内容相匹配,结尾升华了一个高度。

拒绝桂冠诗人头衔的菲利普·拉金认为唯一能延续的就是爱。温迪坦言自己喜欢拉金的诗歌,特别是拉金的《初见》,该诗二十多年来一直是她最喜欢的诗歌之一。

除了自己的独创,温迪还擅长模仿诸如锡德尼、莎士比亚、艾略特、拉金、休斯等著名诗人的诗歌,特别是对锡德尼、莎士比亚等诗人的模仿,充分显示了她韵律方面的卓越才华,给英语诗坛吹进了一股清新的风。

5.真实的情感

有人认为诗歌应是哲学的另一种形式,有人认为诗歌应是情感的流露。作为英国当代诗坛一位备受尊敬的女诗人,在诗歌创作上,温迪强调一种纯粹、真实的感情。《泰晤士报》这样评述道:值得指出的是,如果没有真实的情感,她的笑话也不会如此令人回味。温迪说,一个诗人无论是抒写自己的生活,还是记录公众事件或对周遭世界的反应,倘若他有意或无意地不诚实,诗歌就不会成功。温迪的诗行采撷她对日常生活的细致观察和独特感受,甚至是成长过程中的记录。谈到成为诗人的理由,她说"是禁不住"。的确,温迪禁不住要"告诉真相"。温迪借奥地利作曲家弗朗兹·舒伯特的话说:"我的目的就是将我的所思所想告知世界。"她说:"诗歌依赖灵感,灵感来源于生活、电影、书籍或是与朋友间的谈话,有些灵感也来自对生活的感悟。"

她的诗歌《火车上》描绘彼此熟知的恋人（抑或一对相互厮守的老夫妻）日常生活中屡见不鲜的一幕——相濡以沫的幸福和温情。这种真实的情感正是源于内心深处对琐碎生活的感悟。

我正读的书
摊在我的膝上。你睡了

窗外很美
田野、精致的湖泊和光秃秃的树枝
尽沉醉于二月的阳光里
每一辆停泊的车都是一片闪亮的马赛克

在这悠悠的灿烂时刻
你的手在我手里
依然暖和，依然暖和

这首温馨的小诗应验了德国学者黑格尔的话"诗就是清风吹过竖琴发出的一阵短暂的乐音"。艺术源于生活。温迪说："我非常热爱诗歌，也享受写诗的过程，诗歌使我的生活变得多姿多彩，也让我对生活的感受更加深刻。"她的《又见情人节》有异曲同工之妙：

…………
我们地老天荒的爱情，已不再新奇，也不再疯狂
你知道我是你的，我知道你是我的
这样说着已很浪漫

> 我最亲爱的爱人，我心爱的情人

没有华丽的辞藻，真挚的情感由清新直白的语言道出，让人倍感温馨。《独立报》将温迪和拒绝桂冠诗人头衔的英国诗人菲利普·拉金相提并论，说他们都是用简洁的语言表达着强烈的情感，有时让读者潸然泪下。温迪坦言："爱是对另一半的关心胜过自己，为了使对方开心，有时候我们也要做出一些牺牲。我与丈夫相处多年，老夫老妻已很难制造出年轻时的青春浪漫，但是我们的爱情却像涓涓细流一样，温暖质朴。"

宋人葛立方说："落其纷华，乃造平淡之境。"当激情冷却，爱情升华为亲情，我们需要的正是这种相濡以沫。

> 你若问我"有什么新鲜事？"我无言以对
> 除了花园在生长
> 我昨天感冒了，今天好多了
> 我很乐意一切安然如故
> 是的，他还和平时一样
> 吃吃、睡睡、打打呼噜
> 我忙我的，他忙他的
> 这的确很无聊
>
> 在不堪回首的过去，我经历了太多戏剧性的变故：
> 泪水和激情——我耗了满满一箱
> 没消息就是好消息，希望长此下去
> 没有大事发生，我已十分感激
> 我就是一颗索然无味的卷心菜，幸福地自成世界
> ……………

今生就一个心愿：
就是继续，继续这样无聊下去

宋代文学家苏轼说"绚烂之极，归于平淡"。的确，没消息就是好消息，平平淡淡才是真。这首创于温迪成名后的《无聊下去》唱出所有甘于平淡的老夫老妻的心曲。诗人用平实的语言表达了真实的情感——对爱情婚姻和现实生活的满足。温迪的诗歌创作随着自己的心意，不谄媚附庸，不矫揉造作。正如《星期日电讯报》所言，温迪诗歌的一个大特色就是真。正因为温迪的诗大胆、直率，甚至一针见血，她被认为是诗人中的奇才、大写的诗人。当有人评价她的诗歌比较搞笑时，她回应道："创作是为了逗乐？这建议令人惊愕！／我创作为了使一些人焦虑、难过，让其消化道堵塞。"

结束语

不同于其他诗人晦涩难懂的诗歌，温迪的诗简洁明了，韵律优美，富有真情。她敏锐的洞察力和她对语言的驾驭力使她睿智、诙谐且饱含真情的诗歌深受读者喜欢，连一些很少读诗的读者都喜欢读她的诗，她的诗集占据获奖榜单长达十六年之久。她的诗《午饭后》被谱曲，即歌曲《滑铁卢桥》。她创作的俳句也被谱成歌曲。

温迪的作品拥有大量的读者，但研究她作品的专家和学者并不多，这也许应了荣获诺贝尔文学奖的法国小说家阿尔伯特·加缪的话，"表达清晰的作者拥有读者，表达晦涩的作者拥有评论者"。

参考文献：

[1] COPE WENDY. *Two Cures for Love*[M]. London: Faber and Faber Limited, 2008.

[2] COPE WENDY. *Making Cocoa for Kingsley Amis*[M]. London: Faber and Faber Limited, 1986.

[3] COPE WENDY. *Life, Love and The Archers*[M]. London: Hodder& Stoughton Ltd, 2014.

[4] COPE WENDY. [Z]. https://en.wikipedia.org/wiki/ Wendy_Cope, 2018-4-7.

[5] 方琼玟. 英国著名女诗人温迪·可普的另类浪漫[Z]. http：//www.chinanews.com/cul/2011/07-24/3204920.shtml.

[6] 钱青. 英国十九世纪文学史[M]. 北京：外国文学与研究出版社，2006.

[7] *Poetic Asessment NINE: Wendy Cope Acumen* [J]. Garry Cambridge. September 26, 1996.

[8] COPE WENDY. *Family Values* [M]. London: Faber and Faber Limited, 2011.

[9] 温迪·蔻普. [Z]. https://baike.baidu.com/item/%E6%B8%A9%E8%BF%AA%E5%8F%AF%E6%99%AE/107082847f=aladdin, 2016-10-27.

[10] 范秀华，朱朝晖. 英美诗歌鉴赏入门[M]. 东华大学出版社，2007.

[11] COPE WENDY. *Worry*[Z]. https://www.poemhunter.com/poem/you-said-i-said/#content, 2010-5-25.

[12] COPE WENDY. *Anecdotal Evidence*[M]. London: Faber and Faber Limited, 2018.

[13] 曾心，王珂. 曾心小诗500首[M]. 东南大学出版社，2017.

[14] COPE WENDY. *Serious Concerns*[M]. London: Faber and Faber Limited, 2002.

目录

3	火车上 On a Train	
5	走火入魔 Going Too Far	
7	在莱茵河谷 In the Rhine Valley	
9	该死的男人 Bloody Men	
11	情人 Valentine	
13	无聊下去 Being Boring	
17	痛失男友 Loss	
19	回旋诗 Rondeau Redoublé	
23	如何应付媒体 How to Deal with the Press	
27	给问题定性 Defining the Problem	
29	被画像的模特 The Sitter	
33	谐趣诗 Some More Light Verse	
35	鹦鹉发表自己的观点 Budgie Finds His Voice	
39	谚语式的三节联韵诗 Proverbial Ballade	
43	利物浦的斯特拉格内尔 Strugnell in Liverpool	
51	爱情故事 Love Story	
53	生日卡上的诗 Verse for a Birthday Card	
55	小米勒 Tich Miller	
59	凌晨3点 At 3 a.m.	
61	艾米莉·狄更生 Emily Dickinson	
63	八行两韵诗 Triolet	

65	戒烟 Giving Up Smoking		
67	试写不押韵的诗 An Attempt at Unrhymed Verse		
69	厕所清洁工 The Lavatory Attendant		
73	口信儿 Message		
77	我一定好好的 I'll Be Nice	97	一样的甜蜜 As Sweet
81	郁金香 Tulips	99	关于树的 Arboreal
83	汉普郡的灾难 A Hampshire Disaster	101	康沃的大耳猪 Cornish Lop-eared
87	见你 Seeing You	103	五月 The Month of May
89	斯特拉格内尔的俳句 Strugnell's Haiku	107	一张老相片 On Finding an Old Photograph
91	爱的两副解药 Two Cures for Love	109	书信往来 Exchange of Letters
93	花 Flowers	113	橘子 The Orange
95	午饭后 After the Lunch	115	即将离开 Leaving
		117	名字 Names

119	俳句 Haiku	143	四月 April
121	俳句：没戴眼镜，从卧室的后窗眺看 Haiku: Looking Out of the Back Bedroom Window without My Glasses	145	接着说——筵席还没结束呢 Keep Saying This
		147	不容争辩 You're Not Allowed
123	又一个不幸的选择 Another Unfortunate Choice	151	测验 Quizzes
		153	遗孀 The Widow
125	又见情人节 Another Valentine's Day	155	播音结束 Closedown
127	斯特拉格内尔的《鲁拜集》 From Strugnell's Rubáiyát	159	寄宿女孩 Boarders
131	关于"六八运动"的十四行诗 Sonnet of '68	163	在诗歌会上 At the Poetry Conference
135	九行的八行两韵诗 Nine-line Triolet	165	六十一 Sixty-one
137	斯特拉格内尔十四行诗（为D.M.托马斯） From Strugnell's Sonnets (Ⅴ)	167	第一次约会 First Date
139	斯特拉格内尔的十四行诗（为D.M.托马斯） From Strugnell's Sonnets (Ⅶ)	175	足球 Football

179	丽萨德尔庄园	
	Lissadell	
183	在斯蒂普	
	At Steep	
187	也许	
	Probably	
191	一场朗诵会	
	A Reading	
195	关切	
	Serious Concerns	
197	十四行诗(受莎士比亚十四行诗No. 22的启发而作)	
	Sonnet(inspired by Sonnet 22)	
198	附录	
209	译后记	

On a Train

The book I've been reading

rests on my knee. You sleep.

It's beautiful out there—

fields, little lakes and winter trees

in February sunlight,

every car park a shining mosaic.

Long, radiant minutes,

your hand in my hand,

still warm, still warm.

火车上*

我正读的书
摊在我的膝上。你睡了

窗外很美
田野、精致的湖泊和光秃秃的树枝
尽沉醉于二月的阳光里
每一辆停泊的车都是一片闪亮的马赛克①

在这悠悠的灿烂时刻
你的手在我手里
依然暖和，依然暖和

---

* 请参阅附录P198。
① 直译为每一个停车场都是一幅绚丽的镶嵌画。

Going Too Far

Cuddling the new telephone directory

After I found your name in it,

Was going too far.

It's a safe bet you're not hugging a phone book,

Wherever you are.

走火入魔

当我发现你的名字在新的电话簿里
我就把电话簿搂在怀里
真是走火入魔

无论你在哪里,我敢打赌
你都不会把电话簿搂在怀里

In the Rhine Valley

Die Farben der Bäume sind schön[1]
And the sky's and the river's blue-greys
And the ***Burg***[2], almost lost in the haze.

You're patient. You help me to learn
And you smile as I practise the phrase,
'*Die Farben der Bäume sind schön.*'

October. The year's on the turn—
It will take us our separate ways
But the sun shines. And we have two days.
Die Farben der Bäume sind schön.

[1]***Die Farben der Bäume sind schön***: The colors of the trees are beautiful.

[2]***Burg***: castle.

在莱茵河谷

树的颜色很美
灰蓝的天空和灰蓝的河水也很美
远处的城堡,近乎销匿在薄雾里

你很有耐心地辅导我
当我练这句"Die Farben der Bäume sind schön"①
你笑了

十月,我俩的分水岭——
从此你我南北东西
太阳暖暖地照着,我们还有两天时光
树的颜色很美

①***Die Farben der Bäume sind schön***:德文,意为树的颜色很美。

Bloody Men

Bloody men are like bloody buses —
You wait for about a year
And as soon as one approaches your stop
Two or three others appear.

You look at them flashing their indicators,
Offering you a ride.
You're trying to read the destinations,
You haven't much time to decide.

If you make a mistake, there is no turning back.
Jump off, and you'll stand there and gaze
While the cars and the taxis and lorries go by
And the minutes, the hours, the days.

该死的男人

该死的男人就像那该死的公共汽车
你在站牌下等了近乎一年
但当有一辆驶来时
其他两三辆也一同出现

看着公交车号牌忽闪忽闪
等你搭乘
仓促地浏览车身上的站名
没有太多时间定夺

一旦上错车,车不会倒回
跳下车,你只有立在半道儿眼巴巴地看着
小轿车、出租车和大货车从你身边飞驰而过
飞驰而过的还有时光和岁月

Valentine

My heart has made its mind up

And I'm afraid it's you.

Whatever you've got lined up,

My heart has made its mind up

And if you can't be signed up

This year, next year will do.

My heart has made its mind up

And I'm afraid it's you.

情　人*

我已下定决心
不好意思，就是你了
无论你有何打算
我已下定决心
倘若今年你不能和我牵手
明年也行
我已下定决心
不好意思，就是你了

---

* 请参阅附录P199。

Being Boring

> 'May you live in interesting times.'
> — Chinese curse

If you ask me 'What's new?' I have nothing to say
Except that the garden is growing.
I had a slight cold but it's better today.
I'm content with the way things are going.
Yes, he is the same as he usually is,
Still eating and sleeping and snoring.
I get on with my work. He gets on with his.
I know this is all very boring.

There was drama enough in my turbulent past:
Tears and passion —I've used up a tankful.
No news is good news, and long may it last.
If nothing much happens, I'm thankful.
A happier cabbage you never did see,
My vegetable spirits are soaring.
If you're after excitement, steer well clear of me.
I want to go on being boring.

无聊下去*

> 宁当太平犬,不为乱世人。
> ——中国谚语

你若问我"有什么新鲜事?"我无言以对
除了花园在生长
我昨天感冒了,今天好多了
我很乐意一切安然如故
是的,他还和平时一样
吃吃、睡睡、打打呼噜
我忙我的,他忙他的
这的确很无聊

在不堪回首的过去,我经历了太多戏剧性的变故:
泪水和激情——我耗了满满一箱
没消息就是好消息,希望长此下去
没有大事发生,我已十分感激
我就是一颗索然无味的卷心菜,幸福地自成世界
我就是要安静地像株植物
倘若你要追求刺激,就请远离
我就想这样无聊下去

---

* 请参阅附录P200。

I don't go to parties. Well, what are they for,

If you don't need to find a new lover?

You drink and you listen and drink a bit more

And you take the next day to recover.

Someone to stay home with was all my desire

And, now that I've found a safe mooring,

I' ve just one ambition in life: I aspire

To go on and on being boring.

我不参加聚会。不需要找一个新的爱人
唉，聚会何益？
喝着，听着，你就喝多了
还需要次日恢复体力
我想要的就是和某人待在家里
既然我已找到了停泊的港湾
今生就一个心愿：
就是继续，继续这样无聊下去

Loss

The day he moved out was terrible—

That evening she went through hell.

His absence wasn't a problem

But the corkscrew had gone as well.

痛失男友

他搬出的那天真是糟透了
那个晚上她像跌进地狱一般
他的空缺并非无法对付
但开瓶器怎么也找不见

Rondeau Redoublé

There are so many kinds of awful men —
One can't avoid them all. She often said
She'd never make the same mistake again:
She always made a new mistake instead.

The chinless type who made her feel ill-bred;
The practised charmer, less than charming when
He talked about the wife and kids and fled —
There are so many kinds of awful men.

The half-crazed hippy, deeply into Zen,
Whose cryptic homilies she came to dread;
The fervent youth who worshipped Tony Benn [1]—
'One can't avoid them all,' she often said.

The ageing banker, rich and overfed,
Who held forth on the dollar and the yen —
Though there were many more mistakes ahead,
She'd never make the same mistake again.

The budding poet, scribbling in his den

回旋诗

混账的男人各式各样——
你不可能全躲过。她常说
她再也不犯同样的错：
可她总犯新错

那个没下巴的，她觉着很粗野
这个老练的，她觉得有魅力，但当他谈起
他的妻，他的孩子，便没了踪迹，还奢谈什么魅力
混账的男人各式各样

那个沉醉于禅宗的半疯狂的嬉皮士
他神秘的说教让她恐惧
这个狂热的青年竟膜拜托尼·本①
"你不可能全躲过。"她常说

那个上了岁数的银行家，财力雄厚，营养过剩
张嘴闭嘴就是日元美钞
尽管她曾犯了许多错
她再也没犯同样的错

那个未来的诗人，整日在他的小窝里涂鸦

Odes not to her but to his pussy, Fred;

The drunk who fell asleep at nine or ten —

She always made a new mistake instead.

And so the gambler was at least unwed

And didn't preach or sneer or wield a pen

Or hoard his wealth or take the Scotch to bed.

She'd lived and learned and lived and learned but then

There are so many kinds.

①**Tony Benn:** Anthony Neil Wedgwood Benn (1925-2014), Originally known as Anthony Wedgwood Benn, later as Tony Benn, was a British politician, writer. He was a Member of Parliament for 47 years. Originally a moderate, he was identified as being on the party's hard left from the early 1980s, and was widely seen as a key proponent of democratic socialism with the party.

他的颂歌并非写给她，而是献给他自己的宠物猫弗雷德
这个是醉鬼，每天上午九十点开始昏睡
她总犯一个新错

这个赌徒至少未婚
他不说教，不讥笑，也不耍笔杆子
他不把财富私藏，也不醉醺醺上床
她就这样一直走着，看着；走着，看着
唉，各式各样的混账

①**托尼·本**：原名安东尼·尼尔·韦奇伍德·本（1925—2014），英国政客，作家。当了47年议会议员，起初是温和的中间派，二十世纪八十年代以来被认为是强硬的左翼，民主社会主义的支持者。

How to Deal with the Press

She'll urge you to confide. Resist.
Be careful, courteous, and cool.
Never trust a journalist.

'We're off the record,' she'll insist.
If you believe her, you're a fool.
She'll urge you to confide. Resist.

Should you tell her who you've kissed,
You'll see it all in print, and you'll
Never trust a journalist

Again. The words are hers to twist,
And yours the risk of ridicule.
She'll urge you to confide. Resist.

'But X is nice,' the publicist
Will tell you. 'We were friends at school.'
Never trust a journalist,

Hostile, friendly, sober, pissed,

如何应付媒体

她要你吐露心扉,切莫听她的
要提防,要彬彬有礼,要头脑冷静
绝不要相信媒体记者

"我们只私下谈谈。"她会这么说
如果相信她,你就是傻子
她要你吐露心扉,切莫听她的

如果你告诉她你吻过谁
你会发现很快全世界都知道
绝不要再相信媒体记者

经过她的歪曲
你的言辞会变得可笑至极
她叫你吐露心扉,切莫听她的

"可X很不错哦,"这位媒体人
会这么说,"在学校时我们是朋友。"
绝不要相信媒体记者

敌意或友好,冷静或暴躁

Male or female —— that's the rule.

When tempted to confide, resist.

Never trust a journalist.

无论男女 ——这是原则
叫你吐露心扉,切莫听她的
绝不要相信媒体记者

Defining the Problem

I can't forgive you. Even if I could,

You wouldn't pardon me for seeing through you.

And yet I cannot cure myself of love

For what I thought you were before I knew you.

给问题定性

我不愿原谅你,即便我能
你也不会饶恕我,饶恕看穿了你的我
我无法疗我的情伤
皆因看穿你之前对你的臆想

The Sitter

Vanessa Bell[①], *Nude*, c.1922-3, Tate Britain[②]

Depressed and disagreeable and fat—
That's how she saw me. It was all she saw.
Around her, yes, I may have looked like that.
She hardly spoke. She thought I was a bore.
Beneath her gaze I couldn't help but slouch.
She made me feel ashamed. My face went red.
I'd rather have been posing on a couch
For some old rake who wanted me in bed.
Some people made me smile, they made me shine,
They made me beautiful. But they're all gone,
Those friends, the way they saw this face of mine,
And her contempt for me is what lives on.
Admired, well-bred, artistic Mrs Bell,
I hope you're looking hideous in Hell.

[①]**Vanessa Bell** (1879-1961): An English painter and interior designer, a member of the Bloomsbury Group and the sister of Virginia Woolf (1882-1941).

[②]**Tate Britain:** An art museum in London known from 1897 to

被画像的模特

(瓦内萨·贝尔①,《裸画》,c.1922–3泰特现代美术馆②)

沮丧、乖张、肥胖——
她就是这样看我。她看到的就这样
是的,在她身旁,我也许看起来就这样
她很少说话。她认为我很乏味
在她的目光下,我着实打不起精神
她令我蒙羞,使我脸红
我宁可一直在沙发上为一些恶棍摆姿势
他们需要我在床上
有些人让我欢欣,让我出众
也让我美丽。曾经的朋友,和他们那激励我的眼神
可一切都成为过去
我现在拥有的是她对我的不屑
这个优雅的、众人敬仰、受过良好教育的贝尔夫人
我希望你在地狱里丑恶无比

①**瓦内萨·贝尔**(1879—1961):英国女画家、室内设计师。二十世纪伟大的小说家弗吉尼亚·伍尔芙(1882—1941)的姐姐,是布卢姆茨伯里派成员。
②**泰特现代美术馆**:位于伦敦的英国最大的博物馆

1932 as the National Gallery of British Art and from 1932 to 2000 as the Tate Gallery. It holds the largest collection of British art in the world from 1500 to the present day, and in particular has large holdings of the works of J. M. W. Turner. It is one of the largest museums in the country.

之一。最早名为国立英国艺术美术馆,继而又以创始人亨利·泰特的名字命名。馆内收藏了自公元1500年以来的英国乃至世界的大量艺术珍品,特别是大量的威廉·特纳的艺术品。

Some More Light Verse

You have to try. You see a shrink.
You learn a lot. You read. You think.
You struggle to improve your looks.
You meet some men. You write some books.
You eat good food. You give up junk.
You do not smoke. You don't get drunk.
You take up yoga, walk and swim.
And nothing works. The outlook's grim.
You don't know what to do. You cry.
You're running out of things to try.

You blow your nose. You see the shrink.
You walk. You give up food and drink.
You fall in love. You make a plan.
You struggle to improve your man.
And nothing works. The outlook's grim.
You go to yoga, cry, and swim.
You eat and drink. You give up looks.
You struggle to improve your books.
You cannot see the point. You sigh.
You do not smoke. You have to try.

谐趣诗

你一直在努力。你去看心理医生。
你不停地学习。你阅读。你思考。
你竭力让自己美丽。
你见了一些人。你写了一些书。
你注意饮食。你摒弃垃圾食品。
你不抽烟。你不酗酒。
你练瑜伽、步行、游泳。
可什么都不管用。前景依然暗淡。
你不知究竟该怎么办。你哭了。
所有可以尝试的,你都试了。

你痛哭流涕。你去看心理医生。
你步行。你节食。
你坠入爱河。你制订了计划。
你不遗余力地提升你的男人。
什么都不管用。前景依然暗淡。
你练瑜伽、游泳,又哭又喊。
你开始尽情吃喝。不再顾及形体。
你不遗余力地修改自己的书。
但又不得要领。你叹气。
你不抽烟。你一直在努力。

Budgie Finds His Voice[1]

From *The Life and Songs of the Budgie* by Jake Strugnell[2]

God decided he was tired

Of his spinning toys.

They wobbled and grew still.

When the sun was lifted away

Like an orange lifted from a fruit-bowl

And darkness , blacker

Than an oil-slick,

Covered everything forever

And the last ear left on earth[3]

Lay on the beach

Deaf as a shell

And the land froze

And the seas froze

'Who's a pretty boy then?' [4]Budgie cried.

鹦鹉发表自己的观点①

来自杰克·斯特拉格内尔②的《鹦鹉的生活与歌》

上帝觉着他玩腻了
旋转的玩具
玩具晃了晃,停了下来

挂在天边的太阳
此时就像举在水果盘上的一个橘子

瞬间,比浮油
还黑的夜
笼罩四野

世间的最后一只耳朵③
躺在海滩上
像贝壳一样聋

陆地凝固了
海洋凝固了

远处传来鹦鹉的叫问——"谁是帅气的男孩?"④

①***Budgie Finds His Voice***: A parody of Ted Hughes's book *Crow*. In those poems there is sometimes a change of tone in the last line.

②**Jake Strugnell:** A fictional male poet Wendy invented to write a few of her poems from his point of view.

③**And the last ear left on earth:** This is a parody of Ted Hughes's book *Crow*. In one poem he wrote "And the only face left in the world/Lay broken".

④**Who's a pretty boy then?** : Something English people often teach budgies to say when they keep them as pets.

①**《鹦鹉发表自己的观点》**：该诗是以模仿英国桂冠诗人泰德·休斯《乌鸦》里的诗而创作的。有时候，《乌鸦》里的诗的最后一行会改变语气。

②**杰克·斯特拉格内尔**：女诗人温迪虚构的一个男诗人名字，以他的口吻撰写诗歌。

③**世间的最后一只耳朵**：模仿泰德·休斯《乌鸦》里的一句诗：世间最后一张仰着的脸/破了。

④**谁是帅气的男孩？**：英国人把鹦鹉当宠物养时，喜欢教鹦鹉说"谁是帅气的男孩"？

Proverbial Ballade

Fine words won't turn the icing pink;
A wild rose has no employees;
Who boils his socks will make them shrink;
Who catches cold is sure to sneeze.
Who has two legs must wash two knees;
Who breaks the egg will find the yolk;
Who locks his door will need his keys—
So say I and so say the folk.

You can't shave with a tiddlywink,
Nor make red wine from garden peas,
Nor show a blindworm how to blink,
Nor teach an old racoon Chinese.
The juiciest orange feels the squeeze;
Who spends his portion will be broke;
Who has no milk can make no cheese—
So say I and so say the folk.

He makes no blot who has no ink,
Nor gathers honey who keeps no bees.

谐语式的三节联韵诗*

巧言也难使糖霜由白色变为粉色
野玫瑰没有雇员
袜子煮了就会缩
感冒了就要打喷嚏
有两条腿就需洗两个膝
敲破鸡蛋才能看到蛋黄
锁门的人才需要钥匙开锁——
我这么说，坊间也这么流传着

游戏塑料圆片不能刮脸
红酒不是豌豆酿的
你无法教会无脚蜥蜴眨眼
也教不会老浣熊讲中国话
多汁的橘子愈被榨压
挥霍完钱财的人就会破产
没有牛奶怎会有奶酪——
我这么说，坊间也这么流传着

没墨水就不会有墨渍
无蜜蜂怎会有蜂蜜

---

* 请参阅附录P201。

The ship that does not float will sink;

Who'd travel far must cross the seas.

Lone wolves are seldom seen in threes;

A conker ne'er becomes an oak;

Rome wasn't built by chimpanzees—

So say I and so say the folk.

浮不起的船会沉没

远游的人必须跨海过河

孤独的狼难见三五成群

七叶树的果长不出橡木

罗马不是大猩猩建的——

我这么说,坊间也这么流传着

Strugnell in Liverpool[①]

For Allen Ginsberg[②], Charlie Parker[③], T.S. Eliot[④], Paul McCartney[⑤], Marcel Proust[⑥] and all the other great men who have influenced my writing

waking early*
listening to
birdsong watching
the curtains brighten
like a shirt
washed in Omo
feeling the empty
space beside me
thinking of you

crawling out of
bed searching
for my glasses
piles of clothing
on the carpet
none of it yours

---

* 原诗句首字母为小写,后同。——译注

利物浦的斯特拉格内尔①

献给艾伦·金斯伯格②、查理·帕克③、T.S.艾略特④、保罗·麦卡特尼⑤、马塞尔·普鲁斯特⑥和其他影响我创作风格的伟人们。

早早醒了
听
鸟鸣
看
窗帘
恰似浸在奥妙洗涤剂里的衬衫
白了
身边空荡荡的
想起你

爬起来
摸
眼镜
地板上
一堆衣服里
没你的

alone in the toilet

with the Harpic

and the Andrex

thinking of you

eating my cornflakes

plastic flowers on

the windowsill green

formica table lovesong

on the radio bacteria

in the drainpipe

thinking of you

going

up

stairs

again

and

getting

dressed

think-

ing

of

you

一个人
与瑕辟洁厕剂
和安得利卫生纸
待在卫生间
想起你
吃着玉米片
窗台上的塑料花
贴有塑料贴面的绿餐桌
收音机里的情歌
下水道里的细菌
想起你

又
走
上
楼
穿
上
衣

想
起
了
你

thinking

of you your pink

nylon panties

and your blue

nylon bra

Body Mist

hairsmell of Silvikrin

shampoo and your white

nylon panties

thinking of you

①**Strugnell in Liverpool:** This poem is a parody of a poem by Adrian Henri (1932-2000). He was a British poet and painter influenced by the French Symbolist school of poetry and surrealist art.

②**Allen Ginsberg:** Irwin Allen Ginsberg (1926-1997), one of the leading figures of the Beat Generation during the 1950s. He vigorously opposed militarism, economic materialism and sexual repression. He is best known for his poem *Howl*.

③**Charlie Parker :** (1920-1955), also known as Yardbird and Bird, was an highly influential American jazz saxophonist and composer and a leading figure in the development of bebop.

想起

你的

　　粉尼龙内裤

　　蓝尼龙胸罩

你的保湿喷雾剂

和你用 Silvikrin 牌洗发水

洗发后的味道

还有你的

　　白尼龙内裤

想起你

①**利物浦的斯特拉格内尔**：该诗是诗人温迪仿写英国诗人艾德礼安·亨利的诗。艾德礼安（1932—2000）是英国诗人和画家。他深受法国象征主义诗歌和超现实主义艺术的影响。

②**艾伦·金斯伯格**：欧文·艾伦·金斯伯格（1926—1997），美国二十世纪五十年代垮掉一代的领军人物。他强烈反对战争，反对物质至上，反对性压抑。代表作《嚎叫》。

③**查理·帕克**：（1920—1955），绰号大鸟，是美国颇有影响力的爵士萨克斯演奏家和作曲家。他是比波普爵士乐发展的领军人物。根据其生平改编的

④**T. S. Eliot:** Thomas Stearns Eliot (1888—1965), an English poet, playwright, literary critic and a leader of the Modernist movement in poetry. He was awarded the Nobel Prize in 1948. His masterpieces include *The Love Song of J.Alfred Prufrock, The Waste land,Four Quartets, Murder in the Cathedral*, etc.. *The Waste Land*, is arguably the most important poem of the whole twentieth century.

⑤**Paul McCartney:** Sir James Paul McCartney, CH, MBE (born 18 June 1942), is an English singer-songwriter, multi-instrumentalist, and composer. He gained worldwide fame as the bass guitarist and singer for the rock band the Beatles, widely considered the most popular and influential group in the history of pop music. His songwriting partnership with John Lennon was the most successful of the post-war era.

⑥**Marcel Proust:** Valentin Louis Georges Eugène Marcel Proust (1871-1922) was a French novelist, critic, and essayist best known for his monumental novel À la recherche du temps perdu (*In Search of Lost Time*); earlier rendered as *Remembrance of Things Past*). He is considered by critics and writers to be one of the most influential authors of the 20th century.

电影《火鸟重生》(*Bird*)获多项国际大奖。

④**T.S.艾略特**：托马斯·斯特尔那斯·艾略特（1988—1965），英国诗人、剧作家和文学评论家，现代派诗歌运动的领袖。他于1948荣获诺贝尔文学奖。代表作包括《阿尔弗瑞德·普罗弗洛克的情歌》《荒原》《四个四重奏》《大教堂凶杀案》等。《荒原》被视为英美现代诗歌的里程碑。

⑤**保罗·麦卡特尼**：詹姆斯·保罗·麦卡特尼生于1942年6月18日，英国歌手、词曲作者、多种乐器的演奏家。他以甲壳虫摇滚乐队的歌手和低音吉他手而闻名世界。该乐队被认为是流行音乐史上最受欢迎和最有影响力的乐队。他和创作搭档约翰·列侬的合作被认为是战后音乐界最成功的合作。

⑥**马塞尔·普鲁斯特**：瓦伦丁·路易斯·乔治·尤金·马塞尔·普鲁斯特（1871—1922），法国小说家、评论家、散文家。以其代表作《追忆逝水年华》闻名世界。被公认是二十世纪影响最大的作家之一。

Love Story

I thought you'd be a pushover;
I hoped I wouldn't hurt you.
I warned you this was just a fling
And one day I'd desert you.

So kindly in your spectacles,
So solid in your jacket,
So manly in your big white car
That must have cost a packet.

I grew to like you more and more—
I didn't try to hide it.
Fall in love with someone nice? —
I'd hardly ever tried it.

The course of true love didn't run
Quite the way I'd planned it.
You failed to fall in love with me—
I couldn't understand it.

爱情故事

料定你会轻易地跪在我的石榴裙下
着实不想伤你
于是提醒你这只是一时的纵欲
不久我们就会南北东西

你镜片后面的眼神　温存
你夹克里的身体　健壮
你开着宽大的白色轿车　器宇轩昂
那车一定耗了一大笔款项

愈来愈喜欢你
感情的事我不会隐匿
与一个合适的人恋爱?
还没试过呢,从前

爱
未能如愿启程
你竟没有爱上我——
不懂

Verse for a Birthday Card

Many happy returns and good luck.

When it comes to a present, I'm stuck.

If you weren't far away

On your own special day,

I could give you a really nice glass of lager.

生日卡上的诗

往日重现,祝福你
在这个特别的日子里
没礼物送你
倘若你在身边
请你喝一大杯醇香的啤酒

Tich Miller

Tich Miller wore glasses
with elastoplast-pink frames
and had one foot three sizes larger than the other.

When they picked teams for outdoor games
she and I were always the last two
left standing by the wire-mesh fence.

We avoided one another's eyes,
stooping, perhaps, to re-tie a shoelace,
or affecting interest in the flight

of some fortunate bird, and pretended
not to hear the urgent conference:
'Have Tubby!,' 'No, no, have Tich!'

Usually they chose me, the lesser dud,
and she lolloped, unselected,
to the back of the other team.

At eleven we went to different schools.

小米勒*

小米勒戴副
粉色的弹塑框架眼镜
她的一只脚比另一只脚大两倍

当他们在户外组队做游戏时
站在栅栏边的她和我
总是被挑剩下的两个

我俩谁也不看谁
或弯下腰,把鞋带再系一系
或貌似饶有兴致地看那幸福飞翔的鸟

佯装
没听到那急切的争吵
"要胖胖!""不,不,要小小!"

通常这时他们选我,击球我并非一窍不通
而没被选上的她
踉跄地跟在另一队的后面

十一岁时,我俩上了不同的学校

---

* 请参阅附录P202。

In time I learned to get my own back,

sneering at hockey-players who couldn't spell.

Tich died when she was twelve.

我终于能以牙还牙
把会打曲棍球而不会拼写的他们嘲笑

小米勒却死了,那年她刚十二岁

At 3 a.m.

the room contains no sound

except the ticking of the clock

which has begun to panic

like an insect, trapped

in an enormous box.

Books lie open on the carpet.

Somewhere else

you're sleeping

and beside you there's a woman

who is crying quietly

so you won't wake.

凌晨3点

室内一片静寂

除了嘀嗒嘀嗒的闹钟

闹钟

仿佛一只困在大盒子里的昆虫

已感到惶恐

摊开的书散在地毯上

你在某处

熟睡

身旁一个女人

在饮泣

而你却不醒

Emily Dickinson[1]

Higgledy-piggledy
Emily Dickinson
Liked to use dashes
Instead of full stops.

Nowadays, faced with such
Idiosyncrasy,
Critics and editors
Send for the cops.

[1]**Emily Dickinson(1830-1886):** One of the two foremost American poets of the 19th century (The other is Walt Whitman). She has become widely acknowledged as an innovative, proto-modernist poet. She who never married became known as "the nun of Amherst." Emily Dickinson has come to be hailed as perhaps the greatest female poet since Sappho. In total, she wrote over 1800 poems.

艾米莉·狄更生①

体例混乱
艾米莉
喜欢用破折号
替代句号

当下,倘若
评论家和编辑
见到这癖好
他们会报警

①**艾米莉·狄更生**(1830—1886):美国十九世纪最著名的两位诗人之一(另一位是惠特曼)。美国现代主义诗歌的先驱。终身未嫁,文学史上称她为"阿默斯特的女尼"。被誉为古希腊萨福以来西方最杰出的女诗人。创作诗歌1800多首。

Triolet

I used to think all poets were Byronic①—
Mad, bad and dangerous to know.
And then I met a few. Yes it's ironic—
I used to think all poets were Byronic.
They're mostly wicked as a ginless tonic
And wild as pension plans. Not long ago
I used to think all poets were Byronic—
Mad, bad and dangerous to know.

①**Byronic:** characteristic of or resembling Byron or his poetry, this is, contemptuous of and rebelling against conventional morality, or defying fate, or possessing the characteristics of Byron's romantic heroes, or imitating his dress and appearance.

八行两韵诗

我曾以为诗人都是拜伦式的[①]——
疯疯癫癫、乖戾叛逆,结交很危险
后来见了几个。是的,挺讽刺的——
我曾以为诗人都是拜伦式的
和不含杜松子酒的滋补品一样缺德——
像养老金计划一样野蛮
不久前我还以为诗人都是拜伦式的——
疯疯癫癫、乖戾叛逆,结交很危险

①**拜伦式的**:具有或类似于拜伦或拜伦诗歌的特征,即蔑视并且反抗传统道德,挑战命运,或具有拜伦浪漫主义英雄的特点,模仿他的衣着、外貌等。

Giving Up Smoking

There's not a Shakespeare sonnet

Or a Beethoven quartet

That's easier to like than you

Or harder to forget.

You think that sounds extravagant?

I haven't finished yet—

I like you more than I would like

To have a cigarette.

戒 烟

无论是莎翁的十四行
还是贝多芬的四重唱
哪个也没你更令人痴迷
或更令人难忘

你觉着我故弄玄虚?
我还没说完——
我喜欢你胜过
想抽一支烟

An Attempt at Unrhymed Verse

People tell you all the time,

Poems do not have to rhyme.

It's often better if they don't

And I'm determined this one won't .

                    Oh dear.

Never mind, I'll start again.

Busy, busy with my pen…cil.

I can do it, if I try—

Easy, peasy, pudding and gherkins.

Writing verse is so much fun,

Cheering as the summer weather,

Makes you feel alert and bright,

'Specially when you get it more or

less the way you want it.

试写不押韵的诗

人们总说
诗歌未必要押韵
说不押韵似乎更好
那么这首我就尽量不押
　　　　　哦,天呐!

我又重新开始了,没关系
忙啊,忙着挥——笔
我可以的,如果我竭力——
呵,小菜一碟,挺容易

写诗的滋味真妙
如明朗的夏日
就觉着自己才思敏捷
特别是当或多或少地找到
感觉

The Lavatory Attendant

> I counted two and seventy stenches
> All well defined and several stinks!
>
> —Coleridge[1]

Slumped on a chair, his body is an S
That wants to be a minus sign.

His face is overripe Wensleydale[2]
Going blue at the edges.

In overalls of sacerdotal white
He guards a row of fonts

With lids like eye-patches. Snapped shut
They are castanets. All day he hears

Short-lived Niagaras[3], the clank
And gurgle of canescent cisterns.

When evening comes he sluices a thin tide
Across sand-coloured lino,

厕所清洁工

我准确地数出了七十二种臭气
还有其他说不上名字的怪味
　　　　　——柯勒律治①

瘫坐在椅子上的他,像个S
一个渴望舒展为减号的S

他衰老的脸仿佛熟过的文斯勒德奶酪②
侧面布满斑点

身着圣洁的白色工装
他看护着一排圣洗池般神圣的马桶

眼罩似的马桶盖,啪啪盖上
就像舞曲里的响板打响

整日,听着尼亚加拉③短暂的哗哗、咣当
和白色水箱里的汩汩清唱

夜幕降临,他开启小溪
把地板上的沙色油布冲洗

Turns Medusa④ on her head

And wipes the floor with her.

①**Coleridge:** Samuel Taylor Coleridge (1772 –1834), was an English poet, literary critic, philosopher and theologian, who with his friend William Wordsworth, was a founder of the Romantic Movement in England and a member of the Lake Poets. He wrote the poems *The Rime of the Ancient Mariner and Kubla Khan*. He was a major influence on Ralph Waldo Emerson and American transcendentalism.

②**Wensleydale:** A style of cheese originally produced in Wensleydale, North Yorkshire, England which is white, tangy, crumbly and slightly moist, with distinctive veins of blue mold. Now it is mostly made in large commercial creameries throughout the UK.

③**Niagaras:** Niagara is the name of an automatic flushing mechanism widely used in British public lavatories. It borrows from Niagara Falls standing between Canada and the United States. Niagara Falls is famed both for its beauty and as a valuable source of hydroelectric power.

④**Medusa:** A monster in Greek mythology. She had the face of an ugly woman with snakes instead of hair.

再转动着美杜莎④那爬满毒蛇的头——拖把
把地板擦

①柯勒律治：塞缪尔·泰勒·柯勒律治（1772—1834），英国浪漫主义诗人、文学评论家，哲学家、神学家，与其朋友华兹华斯同为"湖畔诗人"成员，是英国浪漫主义的奠基人物。代表作有《古舟子咏》《忽必烈汗》等。他的理论思想对爱默生及美国超验主义有着重要的影响。

②文斯勒德奶酪：一种风味独特的奶酪，最早的产地是英国约克郡文斯勒德。该奶酪的独特风格是嫩白、酥软，奶油味浓，带有青霉点。现在这种奶酪由英国大型商业奶油公司制成。

③尼亚加拉：一种广泛用于英国公共卫生间的自动冲水装置。该商品名借鉴位于加拿大和美国之间的尼亚加拉大瀑布，其因美丽的自然风光及极具价值的水能而闻名。

④美杜莎：希腊神话中的一个女妖，其头发由无数条小蛇组成，面貌丑陋。

Message

Pick up the phone before it is too late
And dial my number. There's no time to spare—
Love is already turning into hate
And very soon I'll start to look elsewhere.

Good, old-fashioned men like you are rare—
You want to get to know me at a rate
That's guaranteed to drive me to despair.
Pick up the phone before it is too late.

Well, wouldn't it be nice to consummate
Our friendship while we've still got teeth and hair?
Just bear in mind that you are forty-eight
And dial my number. There's no time to spare.

Another kamikaze love affair?
No chance. This time I'll have to learn to wait
But one more day is more than I can bear—
Love is already turning into hate.

Of course, my friends say I exaggerate

口信儿

快拿起电话
拨我的号码。没时间啦——
爱要转为怨
不久,我就会寻伴天涯

你这样既优雅又传统的男人实属罕见——
你想结识我,可你那速度
能把我逼疯
快拿起电话,别耽搁啦

趁你我还有一口白牙,一头黑发
还不赶紧将我们的友谊升华?
要知道你已四十八
快拨我的号码,别磨叽啦

又是一段冒险的风流韵事?
不可能。这次我要学会沉着
但再多等一天,我就会受不了——
爱正转为怨

当然啦,朋友们说我太夸张

And dramatize a lot. That may be fair

But it is no fun being in this state

And very soon I'll start to look elsewhere.

I know you like me but I wouldn't dare

Ring you again. Instead I'll concentrate

On sending thought-waves through the London air

And, if they reach you, please don't hesitate—

Pick up the phone.

太多变,也许有道理
但当下的局面实在无趣
不久我就会寻伴天涯

我知道你喜欢我,但我
不敢再给你打电话。我只有竭力地
通过伦敦的空气向你发送我思念的波
倘若你收到了,切莫犹豫——
请立刻抓起电话,拨我的号码

I'll Be Nice

I'll be nice to you and smile—
It's easy for a man to win—
But I'll hate you all the while.

I shall go the extra mile
And condone your every sin—
I'll be nice to you and smile.

You will think I like your style;
You'll believe I've given in
But I'll hate you all the while.

Safe as an atomic pile,
Good as nitroglycerine,
I'll be nice to you and smile.

I'll say hypocrisy is vile
And give a reassuring grin
But I'll hate you all the while.

Set against my wits and guile,

我一定好好的

我会对你好,冲着你笑——
男人赢 的确很容易——
但我会一直记恨你

我会更多地付出
原谅你所有的罪过
我会对你好,对你笑——

你以为我喜欢你的风格
你坚信你征服了我
但我一直记恨你

像核反应堆一样安全
像炸药一样完好
我会对你好,对你笑

我会说虚伪是卑鄙的
我咧开嘴大笑,让你安心
但我一直记恨你

与我的智慧和心计抗衡

Manly strength won't save your skin.

I'll be nice to you and smile

But I'll hate you all the while.

男性的力气也救不了你
我会对你好，对你笑
但我一直记恨你

Tulips

Months ago I dreamed of a tulip garden,
Planted, waited, watched for their first appearance,
Saw them bud, saw greenness give way to colours,
Just as I'd planned them.

Every day I wonder how long they'll be here.
Sad and fearing sadness as I admire them,
Knowing I must lose them, I almost wish them
Gone by tomorrow.

郁金香

几个月前,我曾梦见一个郁金香花园
跟我设计的一模一样
我把它们种下,守着,看它们最初的模样
看它们发芽,看绿叶里绽出绚烂的花

现在,每天都在想着它们还能待多久
因为太爱了,我悲伤的心满是恐惧
知道终要失去,我几乎希望它们
明天就离去

A Hampshire[1] Disaster

'Shock was the emotion of most'

Hampshire Chronicle, 13 May 1994

When fire engulfed the headquarters

Of the Royal Winchester[2] Golf Club

In the early hours of Wednesday morning,

Shock was the emotion of most.

But fear had been the emotion

Of some who saw the flames, and admiration

For the courage and skill of the firefighters

Was another emotion felt.

At the loss of so much history—

Cups, trophies, and honours boards—

Sadness is now the emotion

Of many Winchester golfers.

Stoical resignation was the emotion

Of the club captain. As he told the *Chronicle*

'The next procedure will be to sort out the insurance.

汉普郡①的灾难

"震惊是当时最强烈的感受"
《汉普郡周报》，1994年5月13日

当大火在星期三的凌晨
吞没了温彻斯特②
皇家高尔夫俱乐部总部
震惊是当时最强烈的感受

目睹熊熊大火的人们最直观的感受
是恐惧
还有为消防战士的技能和勇气
而迸发的另一感受——钦佩

大火吞噬了优胜杯、奖杯和荣誉榜——
辉煌的历史篇章
温彻斯特高尔夫球手们的感受
是悲伤

俱乐部部长的感受是
坦然面对。他告诉《汉普郡周报》
"下一步是整理出保险单

Life must go on.'

(Nobody was hurt in the fire at the Royal Winchester Golf Club in 1994.)

①**Hampshire:** A county on the southern coast of England in the United Kingdom, whose county town is Winchester. Hampshire is notable for housing the birthplaces of the Royal Navy, British Army, and Royal Air Force.

②**Winchester:** A city and the county town of Hampshire, the former capital city of England.

生活仍要继续"

（1994年温彻斯特皇家高尔夫俱乐部的火灾无人伤亡。）

①**汉普郡**：位于英国英格兰南部的一个郡，是英国人口密集的郡之一，首府是温彻斯特。是英国皇家海军、英国陆军及皇家空军的诞生地。

②**温彻斯特**：汉普郡的首府，是英格兰于伦敦之前的古都。

Seeing You

Seeing you will make me sad.

I want to do it anyway.

We can't relive the times we had—

Seeing you will make me sad.

Perhaps it's wrong. Perhaps it's mad.

But we will both be dead one day.

Seeing you will make me sad.

I have to do it anyway.

见 你

见到你我就心碎
但我还是想见你
往日无法重温,我知道——
见到你我就心碎
这或许是犯傻,或许是发疯
但终有一天我们都会死去
见到你我就心碎
但我还是要见你

Strugnell's Haiku[1]

I

The cherry blossom

In my neighbour's garden—Oh!

It looks really nice.

II

The leaves have fallen

And the snow has fallen and

Soon my hair also…

III

November evening:

The moon is up, rooks settle,

The pubs are open.

[1] **Haiku:** A very short form of Japanese poetry. It is a short three-line poem with 5-7-5 syllable structure that uses sensory language to capture a feeling of image.

斯特拉格内尔的俳句①

I

开在邻家
花园里的樱花——
啊,真美!

II

叶凋
雪落
还有不久后我的发……

III

十一月的夜晚:
月如钩,鸦无声
酒吧都开着

①俳句:日本的一种古典短诗。它以三句5—7—5共17个音组成。其特点是用准确、形象的语言捕捉一种意象。

Two cures for love

1. Don't see him. Don't phone or write a letter.
2. The easy way: get to know him better.

爱的两副解药

1. 不见他。不给他打电话,也不写信给他。
2. 最简便的办法:再了解了解他。

Flowers

Some men never think of it.
You did. You'd come along
And say you'd nearly brought me flowers
But something had gone wrong.

The shop was closed. Or you had doubts —
The sort that minds like ours
Dream up incessantly. You thought
I might not want your flowers.

It made me smile and hug you then.
Now I can only smile.
But, look, the flowers you nearly brought
Have lasted all this while.

花

有些男人从没想起过
你想到了。你来看我
还说你几乎要给我买些花
但后来出了个岔

商店门关了。或者你没把握——
我们相似的心智总是
不停地设想。你想
也许我并不需要你的花

听了你的话,我笑了,给了你一个拥抱
此刻我只能笑笑
但是,你瞧,你几乎要买来的花
一直绽放着

After the lunch

On Waterloo Bridge, where we said our goodbyes,
The weather conditions bring tears to my eyes.
I wipe them away with a black woolly glove
And try not to notice I've fallen in love.

On Waterloo Bridge I am trying to think:
This is nothing. You're high on the charm and the drink.
But the juke-box inside me is playing a song
That says something different. And when was it wrong?

On Waterloo Bridge with the wind in my hair
I am tempted to skip. *You're a fool.* I don't care.
The head does its best but the heart is the boss —
I admit it before I am halfway across.

午饭后*

滑铁卢桥上，我们挥手道别，
寒风凛冽，泪水满眼。
我用黑羊毛手套将泪拭去，
无法正视对你的爱恋。

滑铁卢桥上，思想无比纠结：
这不算什么，只是你英俊潇洒，我也喝酒了，
心里的点唱机却播放着
一首不同的歌。心曲何时出过错？

滑铁卢桥上，风吹舞着我的头发，
我想雀跃而去。**你个蠢驴。我才不会在意！**
头脑很清醒，却难左右感情——
桥未过半，我承认我已坠入了爱河里。

---

* 请参阅附录P203。

As Sweet

It's all because we're so alike—
Twin souls, we two.
We smile at the expression, yes,
And know it's true.

I told the shrink. He gave our love
A different name.
But he can call it what he likes—
It's still the same.

I long to see you, hear your voice,
My narcissistic object-choice.

一样的甜蜜

都是因为我们太像了
灵魂都一样,我们俩
对这样的表达,我们笑了
是的,准确的表达

我讲给了心理医生,他给我们的爱
起了个不同的名字
随便他怎么称呼——
都一样

我想见你,想听你的声音
我自恋的客体

Arboreal

We hugged a tree last night

And all of us enjoyed it.

Ecstatic, by moonlight,

We hugged a tree last night.

Trees can't put up a fight—

That oak could not avoid it.

We hugged it good and tight—

I hope the tree enjoyed it.

关于树的

昨晚我们拥抱了一棵树
我们都很享受
月光下,我们欣喜若狂
我们昨晚拥抱了一棵树
树木们无法反抗——
橡树也一样
我们紧紧地拥抱了它——
我希望树也很享受

Cornish Lop-eared

A fine white pig of goodly size,

He roots and gobbles from the ground

But when he tries to look around,

His lop ears droop across his eyes.

He doesn't know the world is big

And beautiful. He doesn't try

To wander. He's an easy pig,

Content to stay within his sty.

康沃的大耳猪

一头硕大、壮实的漂亮白猪
在地上拱着,吃着,狼吞虎咽
环视四周时
下垂的大耳遮挡了他的视线

他不知世界很大,很美
他不想劳神去游历。
他是一头乐意被喂养的猪
待在自己的猪舍里,他很惬意

The Month of May

O! the month of May, the merry month of May⋯
　　　　　　　—Thomas Dekker[①] (d. 1632)

The month of May, the merry month of May,
So long awaited, and so quickly past.
The winter is over, and it's time to play.

I saw a hundred shades of green today
And everything that Man made was outclassed.
The month of May, the merry month of May.

Now hello pink and white and farewell grey.
My spirits are no longer overcast.
The winter's over and it's time to play.

Sing 'Fa la la la la', I dare to say,
(Tried being modern but it didn't last)
' The month of May, the merry month of May.'

I don't know how much longer I can stay.
The summers come, the summers go so fast,

五　月

啊，五月，欢乐的五月……
——托马斯·戴克①（Thomas Dekker，死于1632年）

五月，快乐的五月
盼了这么久，却来去匆匆
冬天已过去，此刻是娱乐的好时机

今天我看到上百块儿的绿荫
它们胜过人造的一切
五月，快乐的五月

辞别灰色，开始迎接粉嫩和洁白的花朵
我不再忧郁
冬天已过去，此刻是欢娱的好时机

唱"Fa la la la la"，我敢说
（曾想跟上时代，时代却不停留）
"五月，快乐的五月"

我不知道我能活多久
夏来夏往，匆匆而过

And soon there will be no more time to play.

So *carpe diem*, gather buds, make hay.
The world is glorious. Compare, contrast
December with the merry month of May.
Now is the time, now is the time to play.

①**Thomas Dekker** (1572-1632): An English Elizabethan dramatist and pamphleteer, a versatile and prolific writer. Dekker's poetry enters into popular song when the Beatles included the lyrics of his ballad *Cradle Song* in their 1969 song, *Golden Slumbers*, which was adapted by Paul McCartney for the song of the same name on The Beatles' *Abbey Road* album.

欢娱的时机转瞬即逝

因此啊,采花,晒草,及时欢娱
世界生意盎然。把快乐的五月与
十二月的阴郁比一比
此刻正是,正是欢娱的好时机

①**托马斯·戴克**(1572—1632):英国伊丽莎白时代多才多艺且多产的作家、戏剧家、政治小册子撰写者。甲壳虫乐队的保罗·麦卡特尼1969年将他撰写的民歌《摇篮曲》改编为歌曲《金色梦乡》,在甲壳虫的专辑《阿比大街》里推出,他的诗歌也因此进入了流行歌曲里。

On Finding an Old Photograph

Yalding[①], 1912. My father
in an apple orchard, sunlight
patching his stylish bags;

three women dressed in soft,
white blouses, skirts that brush the grass;
a child with curly hair.

If they were strangers
it would calm me — half-drugged
by the atmosphere — but it does more —

eases a burden
made of all his sadness
and the things I didn't give him.

There he is, happy, and I am unborn.

①**Yalding:** It is a village and civil parish in the Borough of Maidstone in Kent, England.

一张老相片*

耶尔丁①，1912
父亲站在一个苹果园里
穿过树梢的阳光
在他漂亮的袋子上打着补丁

三位身穿白色绸衣的女士
她们的裙子拖在草地
旁边还立着一个卷发孩子

倘若照片上的是陌生人
我一定很平静——甚至有些
漠然——但事实远不止此

那照片让我如释重负
它竟卸下了那因父亲昔日的悲怆和我的无措
而积在我心头的重荷

瞧，他多开心，那时我还没出生呢

①**耶尔丁**：英国肯特郡梅德斯通市下辖的一个村子和教区。诗人出生时，其父五十九岁。

———
＊请参阅附录P204。

Exchange of Letters

'Man who is a serious novel would like to hear from a woman is a poem' —classified advertisement, *New York Review of Books*

Dear Serious Novel,

I am a terse, assured lyric with impeccable rhythmic flow, some apt and original metaphors, and a music that is all my own. Some people say I am beautiful.

My vital statistics are eighteen lines, divided into three-line stanzas, with an average of four words per line.

My first husband was a cheap romance; the second was *Wisden's Cricketers' Almanac*, Most of the men I meet nowadays are autobiographies, but a substantial minority are books about photography or trains.

I have always hoped for a relationship with an upmarket work of fiction. Please write and tell me more about yourself.

Yours intensely
Song of the First Snowdrop

书信往来*

像小说一样严肃的男人很乐意收到浪漫如诗的女人的来信。——《纽约书评》中的分类广告

亲爱的严肃小说:
我是一首简洁而自信的抒情诗,有着流畅的节奏
完美的韵律,新颖贴切的比喻和特有的音乐魅力
有人夸我美丽

重要的是我共十八行
每三行一节,每行约四个词

我的第一任丈夫是低谷的罗曼史
第二任俨然一本《维斯登板球年鉴》
我目前遇到的男人虽有不少是涉及摄影或火车的书
但大部分是自传

一直希望能与顶级小说有些瓜葛。请写信多向我
介绍介绍你。

奔放的
雪莲花之歌

---

* 本诗是在陈韵姿译文的基础上修改润色而成。——译注

Dear Song of the First Snowdrop,

Many thanks for your letter. You sound like just the kind of poem I am hoping to find. I've always preferred short, lyrical women to the kind who go on for page after page.

I am an important 150,000-word comment on the dreams and dilemmas of twentieth-century Man. It took six years to attain my present weight and stature but all the twenty-seven publishers I have so far approached have failed to understand me. I have my share of sex and violence and a very good joke in chapter nine, but to no avail. I am sustained by the belief that I am ahead of my time.

Let's meet as soon as possible. I am longing for you to read me from cover to cover and get to know my every word.

Yours impatiently,
Death of the Zeitgeist[1]

[1]**Death of the Zeitgeist:** Zeitgeist is a German word meaning the spirit of the times. It is often used by English intellectuals. By signing his letter Death of the Zeitgeist, the man reveals that he is a pretentious idiot.

亲爱的雪莲花之歌：
感谢你的来信。听起来你正是我想找的诗
一直以来我喜欢简洁、抒情的女士
胜过那一页接一页的冗长的诗

我是一篇长达15万字的评论
论述二十世纪男性的梦想和困境
我用了六年时间，才有了今天的体重和身形
但是我曾拜访的27家出版社都理解不了我
本文的第9章论述性和暴力
在这一章我还开了一个玩笑，但也是徒劳
我只能告慰自己我超越了时代

若有可能，就让我们即刻见面吧。我非常期待你能够
从头到尾把我一页页品读，读懂我的每一个字。

急不可耐的
时代精神之死[①]

[①]**时代精神之死**：时代精神（Zeitgeist）一词源于德语，是英国知识阶层常用的字眼，此处以"时代精神之死"落款来表明书写人是一个狂妄自大的白痴。

The Orange

At lunchtime I bought a huge orange —
The size of it made us all laugh.
I peeled it and shared it with Robert and Dave —
They got quarters and I had a half.

And that orange, it made me so happy,
As ordinary things often do
Just lately. The shopping. A walk in the park.
This is peace and contentment. It's new.

The rest of the day was quite easy.
I did all the jobs on my list
And enjoyed them and had some time over.
I love you. I'm glad I exist.

橘　子

午饭时我买了个硕大的橘子
那么大的个儿,大家都乐了
我剥了皮把它跟罗伯特和戴夫分吃了
他俩各吃四分之一,我吃了半个

就是那个橘子,让我很开心
就像那些常让我开心的鸡毛蒜皮
特别是近来,购物、闲庭信步
我感到平静和满足。挺新奇的

那天剩下来的时间很是惬意
把该做的都做了
不仅很享受做事,还享受了做事的时光
我爱你。真高兴世间有我

Leaving

(For Dick and Afkham[1])

Next summer? The summer after?

With luck we've a few more years

Of sunshine and drinking and laughter

And airports and goodbyes and tears.

[1]**Dick and Afkham:** Dick Davis who is the English pre-eminent poet, translator and professor, and his Iranian-English wife Afkham Darbandi. Dick translated such great Persian works as *the Shahnameh,* or *Book of Kings* and *The Conference of the Birds,* etc. into English. In all, he has published more than twenty books and numerous honors testify to his talents. He is a Fellow of the Royal Society of Literature.

即将离开
（为迪克和阿夫哈姆而作①）

第二个夏天？之后的又一个夏天？
真幸运，我们又多活了几年
享受着充满阳光、酒水和欢笑的生活
还有机场的挥别与泪眼婆娑

①迪克和阿夫哈姆：英国杰出的诗人、翻译家、教授迪克·戴维斯和他的伊朗裔妻子阿夫哈姆。迪克将波斯语的巨著《列王纪》《群鸟的集会》等译成英语。他共创作和翻译了二十余部作品，荣获诸多殊荣。是英国皇家文学学会会员。

Names

She was Eliza for a few weeks
When she was a baby—
Eliza Lily. Soon it changed to Lil.

Later she was Miss Steward in the baker's shop
And then 'my love', 'my darling', Mother.

Widowed at thirty, she went back to work
As Mrs Hand. Her daughter grew up,
Married and gave birth.

Now she was Nanna. 'Everybody
Calls me Nanna,' she would say to visitors.
And so they did — friends, tradesmen, the doctor.

In the geriatric ward
They used the patients' Christian names.
'Lil', we said, 'or Nanna',
But it wasn't in her file
And for those last bewildered weeks
She was Eliza once again.

名 字

婴儿时,她一度被唤作伊丽莎
伊丽莎·丽莉
不久,又被唤作丽尔

后来她成了面包店的服务员斯图尔德小姐
接着又被唤作"我的爱人""我亲爱的""妈妈"

三十岁守寡,她又以汉德夫人的身份
重新谋生,女儿大了
结了婚,有了孩子

她现在成了奶奶
"每个人都叫我奶奶。"她逢人就说
于是,朋友、商人和医生都叫她奶奶

在老年病房
他们称呼病人的教名
我们唤她"丽尔"或"奶奶"
但这不是她档案里的名字
在那最后几周迷离的日子里
她又被唤作伊丽莎

Haiku

A perfect white wine

is sharp, sweet and cold as this:

birdsong in winter.

俳 句

上等白酒
一定辛辣　醇香　清凉
宛如冬日鸟鸣

Haiku: Looking Out of the Back Bedroom Window without My Glasses

What's that amazing
new lemon-yellow flower?
Oh yes, a football.

俳句：没戴眼镜，从卧室的后窗眺看

那新绽放的奇异的柠檬黄的花
是什么花啊？
哦，是个足球

Another Unfortunate Choice

I think I am in love with A. E. Housman, ①
Which puts me in a worse-than-usual fix.
No woman ever stood a chance with Housman
And he's been dead since 1936.

①**A. E. Housman** (1859-1936): An English poet and scholar regarded as one of the greatest scholars of all time. He attended the Oxford University to study classics where he, a homosexual, fell in love with his roommate Moss Jackson who was not. He never got married. He was appointed Professor at University College London and then at the University of Cambridge. His best known works are *A Shropshire Lad* (1896) as well as *Last Poems* (1922) which was written for Moss. Housman's poetry, was set to music by many British composers.

又一个不幸的选择

我想我爱上了A.E.豪斯曼①先生
这使得我处境更糟
女性在他那儿压根没指望
他1936年就去了天堂

①**A. E. 豪斯曼**(1859—1936):英国诗人、学者,被认为是最伟大的学者之一。他在牛津大学求学期间,爱上了室友莫斯·杰克逊,但莫斯却不是同性恋。这注定了他一生孤寂。他终身未婚。先后执教于伦敦大学、剑桥大学。代表作有诗集《什罗普郡少年》(1896)和《最后的诗》(1922)。《最后的诗》是他为莫斯创作的。他的诗歌被诸多英国音乐人谱曲。

Another Valentine's Day[1]

Today we are obliged to be romantic

And think of yet another valentine.

We know the rules and we are both pedantic:

Today's the day we have to be romantic.

Our love is old and sure, not new and frantic.

You know I'm yours and I know you are mine.

And saying that has made me feel romantic,

My dearest love, my darling valentine.

[1] The original title is "Another Valentine". With the permission from the author, it is entitled "Another Vatentine's Day" in this book.

又见情人节*

今天我们该浪漫一下
再备一份情人节礼物
我们明晓习俗，我们也很迂腐
我们今天浪漫一下
我们地老天荒的爱情，已不再新奇，也不再疯狂
你知道我是你的，我知道你是我的
这样说着已很浪漫
我最亲爱的爱人，我心爱的情人

---

* 该诗原名《另一份情人节礼物》，经诗人温迪许可，在本书中改为现名。

From Strugnell's Rubáiyát

1

Awake! for Morning on the Pitch of Night

Has whistled and has put the Stars to Flight.

The incandescent football in the East

Has brought the splendour of Tulse Hill[1] to Light.

7

Another Pint! Come, loosen up, have Fun!

Fling off your Hang-Ups and enjoy the Sun:

Time's Spacecraft all too soon will carry you

Away - and Lo! the Countdown has begun.

11

Here with a Bag of Crisps beneath the Bough,

A Can of Beer, a Radio -and Thou

Beside me half-asleep in Brockwell Park

And Brockwell Park is Paradise enow.

26

Oh, come with Strugnell — Argument's no Tonic.

One thing's certain: Life flies supersonic.

One thing's certain, Man's Evasion chronic:

The Flower that's blown can never be bionic.

斯特拉格内尔的《鲁拜集》*

1
醒醒！黎明已在黑暗里吹响口哨
把星星放飞
东边发亮的足球
照得塔尔斯山①一片光明

7
来，再干一杯！让心情舒畅
抛开烦忧，享受阳光
时光的飞船即将载你而去
看！倒计时已经开启

11
树下，与一袋薯片在一起
还有一罐啤酒　一台收音机
和半睡半醒的你在布罗克韦尔公园
布罗克韦尔公园就仿佛天堂一般

26
哦，得了吧，斯特拉格内尔——争论于事无补
可以肯定，生命的飞逝是超音速
可以肯定，人们回避真相就像回避慢性病
不愿承认：吹落的花儿不会再绚丽

---

* 请参阅附录P205。

51

The Moving Telex writes and having writ

Moves on; nor all thy Therapy nor Wit

Shall lure it back to cancel half a line

Nor Daz nor Bold wash out a Word of it.

①**Tulse Hill:** A district in South London, England

51

电传文写着传着
你任何的秘诀和智慧
也无法将其召回,将半句删去
宝洁和汰渍也无能为力。

①**塔尔斯山**:英国伦敦南部的一个区。

Sonnet of' 68

The uproar's over, and the calls to fight
For freedom, the Utopian fantasies.
We took a fairground ride to Paradise
And afterwards there's nothing more, goodnight.

The fire burnt out. The veterans, turning grey,
Make legends of the beautiful, wild past.
These will stay with us till we breathe our last:
The red flag and the photograph of **Che**[1].

So many speeches. There's a silence now.
Each of us walks along the city street
Alone, concerned about his daily bread.

We overreached ourselves a little bit.
Euphoria didn't suit us anyhow.
Those who did not outgrow it— they are dead.

(Translated from the German of **Harry Oberländer**[2])

[1]**Che:** Che Guevara(1928-1967), an Argentine Marxist

关于"六八运动"的十四行诗

喧嚣平息,为自由为理想而战的呐喊
也已沉寂
我们从露天广场去了天堂
随后是空寂,晚安

激情已耗尽,头发灰白的老兵
把过去的美丽和狂野演绎为传奇
这一切会一直陪伴我们直至我们停止呼吸:
红色的旗帜和切·格瓦拉①的头像

曾经有太多的演讲,现在却一片沉寂
每个人独自在街上走着
操心今天的面包在哪里

我们是有点不自量力
无论如何,狂热情绪对我们不宜
没有挺过来的他们都已死去

(译自Harry Oberländer②的德语诗)

①切:即切·格瓦拉(1928—1967),阿根廷的

revolutionary, physician, author, guerrilla leader, diplomat, and military theorist. A major figure of the Cuban Revolution, Guevara left Cuba in 1965 to foment revolution abroad. On October 8, 1967, CIA assisted Bolivian troops captured him. And one day later, he was fatally shot by the Bolivian troops. In Bokivia, he acquired his famous nickname, due to his frequent use of the Argentine filler syllable Che. His stylized visage has become a ubiquitous countercultural symbol of rebellion and global insignia in popular culture.

②**Harry Oberländer:** He who wrote the original poem in German in 1980s was a left wing student in Frankfurt in 1968. He got involved in the wave of student protests, sometimes called the movement of '68 in which many student activists were killed. These events pushed some in the student movement toward increasingly extremist violence and the formation of the Red Army Fraction which was responsible for several bombings and murders. Several of the leading members of this group committed suicide in prison in the 1970s. Others were killed before they could be arrested.

马克思主义革命家、医师、作家、游击队长、外交官、军事理论家,古巴革命武装力量的主要缔造者和领导人之一。1965年离开古巴到第三世界进行反对帝国主义的游击战。1967年10月8日,被美国情报局训练的玻利维亚军队逮捕后杀害。他在玻利维亚赢得了他闻名遐迩的绰号"切"(Che)。"Che"在阿根廷和南美的一些地区被广泛使用,类似于汉语中的"喂""喔"等。切·格瓦拉的肖像已成为反传统文化的象征和全球流行文化的标志。

②**Harry Oberländer:** 该诗的原作者哈里·奥伯兰德于二十世纪八十年代用德语创作该诗。哈里是德国法兰克福的左翼学生,1968年他参加了被称为"六八运动"的学潮,学潮中许多学生激进分子被警察射杀或暗杀。学生的死亡事件将学生运动推向暴力抗击,他们成立了赤军团,制造了爆炸和谋杀等血腥事件。二十世纪七十年代,他们中的领导人有的在狱中自杀。其他人在逮捕前被杀。

Nine-line Triolet[1]

Here's a fine mess we got ourselves into,
My angel, my darling, true love of my heart
Etcetera. Must stop it but I can't begin to.
Here's a fine mess we got ourselves into —
Both in a spin with nowhere to spin to,
Bound by the old rules in life and in art.
Here's a fine mess we got ourselves into,
(I'll curse every rule in the book as we part)
My angel, my darling, true love of my heart.

[1]**Nine-line Triolet:** A triolet is supposed to have eight lines. This one breaks the rules a little bit because it is about breaking the rules a little bit.

九行的八行两韵诗[①]

我俩陷入了一场大麻烦,不胜其苦
我的天使,我的宝贝,我的真心爱人
我的……必须悬崖勒马,但我难以举步
我俩陷入了一个大麻烦,不胜其苦——
我俩都昏了头,不知哪儿是归宿
囿于生活和艺术的陈规陋俗
我俩陷入了一个大麻烦,不胜其苦
(如果我俩分手,我要把书里的一切规则咒诅)
我的天使,我的宝贝,我的真心爱人

①**九行的八行两韵诗**:八行诗应该是八行,诗人有意写了九行,为了和诗歌内容吻合——冲破陈规陋俗。

From Strugnell's Sonnets
(For D. M. Thomas[1])

V

How like a sprinter you have turned and run
From me, who'd loved you almost half a year.
The world's become a fridge, there is no sun,
I hardly have the stomach for a beer.
And yet I still have my guitar to strum
And books to read and some fantastic grass
That Tony got me. I sit here and hum
The tunes we used to hear in Norwood bars –
We Are All Slobs, The Muggers' greatest hit—
Do you remember? Once you said to me,
'This is their best since *Education's Shit*',
And I agreed. But I am forty-three
And blew it when I told you I'd much rather
Listen to a jazz band, like your father.

[1]**D. M. Thomas:** Donald Michael Thomas, known as D. M. Thomas (1935–), is a British novelist, poet, playwright and translator graduating from Oxford University in 1959, who is famous for the novel *The White Hotel* (1981).

斯特拉格内尔的十四行诗[1]*
（为D. M. 托马斯[1]）

V

你从我身边跑开就像一个短跑运动员
而我爱你爱了近乎半年
世界成了一个冰箱　没了阳光
我没了喝啤酒的胃口
但仍有吉他弹奏
有要读的书，还有托尼为我修整的
绿茵茵的草坪。我坐在草地上哼唱
我们在诺伍德酒吧常听的
《我们都是懒汉》——"强盗"乐队的经典歌
可记得你曾对我说
"这是他们自那首《教育是放屁》之后最棒的"？
我同意。可我已四十有三了
当我告诉你我像你的老父亲更喜欢爵士乐
一切都被我搞砸了

[1] D. M. 托马斯：唐纳德·迈克尔·托马斯（1935—），英国小说家、诗人、剧作家和翻译家，1959年毕业于牛津大学，因小说《白色旅馆》（1981）出名。

---

* 请参阅附录P206.

From Strugnell's Sonnets
(For D.M Thomas)

VII

At the moment, if you're seen reading poetry in a train,
the carriage empties instantly.
—Andrew Motion[1] in a *Guardian* interview

Indeed 'tis true. I travel here and there
On British Rail a lot. I've often said
That if you haven't got the first-class fare
You really need a book of verse instead.
Then, should you find that all the seats are taken,
Brandish your Edward Thomas[2], Yeats[3] or Pound[4].
Your fellow-passengers, severely shaken,
Will almost all be loath to stick around.
Recent research in railway sociology
Shows it's best to read the stuff aloud:
A few choice bits from Motion's new anthology
And you'll be lonelier than any cloud.
This stratagem's a godsend to recluses
And demonstrates that poetry has its uses.

斯特拉格内尔十四行诗
（为D. M. 托马斯）

VII

> 当下，倘若有人看见你在火车上读诗，车厢顷刻间会空空如也。
> ——安德鲁·莫伸[①]在《卫报》采访中的发言

的确。我经常乘坐英伦地铁
东游西逛。我常说
如果你没有一张一等座车票
那你真的需要有一本诗集
如果你发现座位都已被占满
那就举起你的爱德华·托马斯、叶芝或庞德的诗集[②]
车厢里被剧烈摇晃的其他乘客
就想远离你
对铁路社会学的最新研究显示
最好的办法是大声诵读：
读莫伸新诗集里的片言只语
你会立刻成一朵孤独的云
这是上天赐给隐士的良策
以证明诗歌的用途

①**Andrew Motion** (1952–): An English poet, novelist, and biographer, who was Poet Laureate of the United Kingdom from 1999 to 2009.

②**Edward Thomas:** Philip Edward Thomas (1878–1917), a British poet, essayist and novelist. It was with the encouragement of American poet Robert Frost that he turned to poetry. He is commonly considered a war poet who was killed in the First World War.

Yeats: William Butler Yeats (1865–1939), an Irish poet and one of the foremost figures of 20th-century literature. In 1923, he was awarded the Nobel Prize in Literature. *When you are old* and *The White Birds* are his most popular poems for Chinese readers.

Pound: Ezra Pound (1885–1972), an American poet and critic who actively promoted Imagism, and one of the shaping forces of modernism. Pound's own most famous Imagist poem is *In a Station of the Metro* (1911).

①**安德鲁·莫伸**(1952—)：英国当代诗人、小说家和传记作者。1999至2009年间的英国桂冠诗人。

②**爱德华·托马斯**：菲利普·爱德华·托马斯（1878—1917），英国诗人、散文家和小说家。他因美国诗人罗伯特·弗罗斯特的鼓励，转向诗歌创作。逝于第一次世界大战的他通常被视为战争诗人。

叶芝：威廉·巴特勒·叶芝（1865—1939），爱尔兰诗人，二十世纪最伟大的文学家之一，1923年荣获诺贝尔文学奖。中国读者比较熟悉的诗作有《当你老了》《白鸟》。

庞德：埃兹拉·庞德（1885—1972），美国诗人和文学评论家，积极地促进意象派诗歌运动的发展。现代主义文学的领军人物。庞德最著名的意象诗是《在地铁车站》（1911）。

April

The birds are singing loudly overhead,

As if to celebrate the April weather.

I want to stay in this lovely world forever

And be with you, my love, and share your bed.

I don't believe I'll see you when we're dead.

I don't believe we'll meet and be together.

The birds are singing loudly overhead.

I want to stay in this lovely world forever.

四 月

鸟儿们在头顶高声唱起
仿佛在庆贺四月的好天气
我想和你永驻这美丽的世界里
同床共枕,亲爱的,和你在一起

我不相信我们死了我还能见到你
我不相信我们死后会再次相遇,永不分离
鸟儿们在头顶高声唱起
我想和你永驻这美丽的世界里

Keep Saying This (Excerpts)

Keep saying this and don't forget:
Although you think you're very old,
The party isn't over yet.

You lie awake at night beset
By dread of being dead and cold.
Keep saying this and don't forget:

It doesn't help at all to fret
About what cannot be controlled.
The party isn't over yet.

接着说——筵席还没结束呢（节选）

接着说，别忘了
即使你觉着自己垂垂老矣
筵席还没结束呢

对于死亡和冰冷的恐惧
使你深夜难以入睡
接着说，别忘了——筵席还没结束呢

对于无法掌控的
你焦虑也无用
接着说，筵席还没结束呢

You're Not Allowed

You're not allowed to wonder if it's true:
She loves you very much. She tells you so.
She is the one who knows what's best for you.
She tells you what to do and where to go.

She loves you very much. She tells you so.
That's why she's sending you to boarding school.
She tells you what to do and where to go
And there is no appeal against her rule.

And now she's sending you to boarding school.
She'll upset if you are cross and sad.
And there is no appeal against this rule:
If Mummy is upset, you must be bad.

Her children often make her cross and sad
And then she cries. She cries and sulks all day.
If Mummy is upset, you must be bad.
It's no good saying sorry. You must pay.

You watch her cry. She cries and sulks all day.

不容争辩

不容争辩这是否是真的
她很爱你,她是这么对你说的
只有她知道什么对你最好
让她来告诉你该做什么,该去哪里

她很爱你,她是这么对你说的
这就是为何要把你送到寄宿学校去
让她来告诉你该做什么,该去哪里
不要违背她的旨意

她要把你送到寄宿学校去
如果你表现出不情愿或叛逆,她会难过至极
不要违背她的旨意
让妈妈难过,就是你的错

她的孩子时常叛逆,表现出不情愿
她就大声哭喊,气急败坏地哭喊一整天
让妈妈难过,就是你的错
道歉没用。你必须有所弥补

你亲眼见她大声哭喊,看着她气急败坏地哭喊一整天

You'd make your mother happy , if you could.

It's no use saying sorry. You must pay.

Things will get better, if you're very good.

You'd make your mother happy, if you could.

She is the one who knows what's best for you.

Things will get better, if you're very good.

You're not allowed to wonder if it's true.

你要尽量让妈妈高兴
道歉没用。你必须有所弥补
你若听她的话，一切都好

你要尽量让妈妈高兴
只有她知道什么对你最好
你若听她的话，一切都好
你不容争辩这是否是真的

Quizzes

I'm always glad when there's a quiz
To make my little brain cells fizz.
I get to show off all my wealth
Of general knowledge to myself.

But, any time I'm asked to go
And take part on the radio,
I straight away decline the chance
To show off all my ignorance.

测 验

我一直热衷参加测验
一来活跃大脑
二来把拥有的常识
向自己炫耀

但任何时候请我参加
电台的测验
我都婉言谢绝
我可不想展示我的欠缺

The Widow

I like this piece. I think you'd like it too.

We didn't very often disagree

Back in the days when I sat here with you

And knew that you were coming home with me.

This is the future. It arrived so fast.

When we were young it seemed so far away.

Our years together vanished like a day

At nightfall, sealed forever in the past.

I can't give up on music, just discard

The interest we shared because you died.

And so I come to concerts. But it's hard.

Tonight I'm doing well. I haven't cried.

My head aches. There's a tightness in my throat.

And you will never hear another note.

遗 孀

我喜欢这首曲子,想你也一定喜欢
过去的岁月里我们没有大的分歧
那时我和你就坐在这里
那时的我知道我们会一同回到家里
曾经的未来竟来得如此快
年轻时,未来似乎还很遥远
我们相伴的岁月犹如夜幕降临时的白昼
转瞬即逝,成为永恒的过去
音乐我还时常在听,只是不再听
我们都喜爱的歌,因为你不在了
于是我来听音乐会。但是真的很难
今晚的我表现还不错,我没有哭
但我头很疼,咽喉也难受
因你再也听不到一首曲子了

Closedown

For Alice Arnold[1]

An almost empty building:
Someone, all alone,
Reads the shipping forecast
To a microphone.

Listeners in bedrooms,
Listeners at sea,
Thousands of them, hear her
Speak invisibly,

Hear her through the darkness,
Hear her say goodnight,
Picture her alone there,
Switching off the light.

Is it really like that?
I asked if I could go
And be with the announcer
In the studio.

播音结束

——为爱丽丝·阿诺德[①]而作

在一座空荡荡的大楼里
她独自一人
对着麦克风
预报着海洋天气

卧室里的听众
大海上的听众
成千上万
看不见她,却听着她的播报

穿过漆黑的夜他们聆听她的声音
听她给听众道晚安
想象她独自一人在那里
把灯熄灭

真是如此吗?
我请求能在她播音时
到播音室
去看她,在她旁边待一会儿

And, yes, it's really like that .

Someone, all alone,

Reads the shipping forecast

To a microphone,

Speaks into the darkness,

Says a last goodnight,

Plays the national anthem,

Switches off the light.

①**Alice Arnold:** A female presenter of BBC Radio 4 who did the Shipping Forecast and Closedown on Radio 4.

事实确实如此
她独自一人
对着麦克风
播报着海洋天气

面对黑暗播报
道最后一声晚安
播放国歌
把灯熄灭

①爱丽丝·阿诺德：BBC电台Radio 4 的海洋天气预报播音员。诗人（Wendy）在征得BBC电台老板的同意后专门拜访了她，看她如何播音、看播音室的情形及最后她如何关掉广播。

Boarders

Boarders are better than daygirls.
We never questioned that belief.

We were tough. We could survive
Without our mummies and our daddies,

Not like feeble daygirls.
'Feeble' was our worst insult.

Secretly I knew I was feeble
And lived in fear of being teased.

'Teasing' was our word for bullying.
The bossy girls picked out the victims,

Sometimes turning on one of their own.
Mostly it was verbal;

Now and then a cry went up,
'Chase for Trudy Tipple!'

寄宿女孩

寄宿女孩比走读女孩更有魅力
对此我们从不质疑

我们是女汉子,没有爸妈的照顾
我们也活了过来

我们可不像脆弱的走读女孩
对我们最大的侮辱就是"脆弱"二字

私下里我也脆弱
担心被取乐

"取乐"就是我们说的欺辱
受辱者由飞扬跋扈的大姐大选出

有时也攻击寄宿女孩中的某个
虽然多数情形下只是言语上的

时而一声大喊:
　"追特鲁迪·蒂普尔!"

The girl took flight. The mob
Pursued its human quarry.

I didn't join in. I like to think
It wasn't because I couldn't run.

女孩跑了。这帮暴徒
便开始追逐她们的猎物

我没有参与。当然,
并不是因为我跑不动。

At the Poetry Conference

Melancholy's grape: today I've bitten it.
I'm sad because you live so far away.
I need to write a poem but I've written it
Already: 1989, L.A.

Here we are again and I am crying.
Nothing has changed except that we are old.
We will be far apart when we are dying.
One will go. The other will be told.

By phone or email and it will be over.
The survivor will sit down and weep
And write a poem mourning the ex-lover
And have a drink or two and go to sleep.

That will be that. You see I'm alternating
Two kinds of rhyme, the way you recommend.
I trust you'll give these lines a Grade A rating
And that , of course, will cheer me up no end.

在诗歌会上

今天我品尝了悲伤的葡萄
我很难过,因你住得太远了
我需要写一首诗,可已经写过了:
那是在1989年的洛杉矶

我们又见面了,我哭了
别的都没变,只是我们老了
临终时我们天各一方
一个走了,另一个被告知

通过电话或邮件,然后一切就了结了
活着的那个只能坐下哭泣
写一首悼念亡友的诗
喝上一两杯,然后睡去

仅此而已。你看我诗行的韵律
是两种交替的,你的建议
相信你会给这首诗打个A
当然,这会使我满心欢喜

Sixty–one

Sixty-one and on a diet.

Will I end up thin or fat

When my heart and brain go quiet?

Sixty-one and on a diet

Yet again. My hopes run riot:

Better life, new start—all that.

Sixty-one and on a diet.

Will I end up thin or fat?

六十一

六十一岁的我正在节食
当心脏停止跳动
我终归是个胖子还是瘦子?
六十一岁的我正在节食
再说一遍。我的期望有点肆无忌惮:
变瘦的心愿——过更好生活的新起点
六十一岁的我正在节食
我终归是个胖子还是个瘦子?

First Date

SHE

I said I liked classical music.
It wasn't exactly a lie.
I hoped he would get the impression
That my brow was acceptably high.

I said I liked classical music.
I mentioned Vivaldi[①] and Bach[②].
And he asked me along to this concert.
Here we are, sitting in the half-dark.

I was thrilled to be asked to the concert.
I couldn't decide what to wear.
I hope I look tastefully sexy.
I've done what I can with my hair.

Yes, I'm thrilled to be here at this concert.
I couldn't care less what they play
But I'm trying my hardest to listen
So I'll have something clever to say.

第一次约会

她

我说我喜欢古典音乐
这并非纯粹的谎言
我希望给他的感觉
是我有很深的内涵

我说我喜欢古典音乐
我提到了维瓦尔第[①]和巴赫[②]
于是他邀请我去音乐会
这不,我们正坐在半明半暗之间

被他请去听音乐会的我很激动
甚至不知该如何打扮
我希望在他眼里我既文雅又性感
我把头发也做了

真的,被请去听音乐会的我很激动
根本不在乎演奏的内容
但我竭尽全力聆听
以便我的发言能有点水平

When I glance at his face it's a picture

Of rapt concentration. I see

He is totally into this music

And quite undistracted by me.

①**Vivaldi:** Antonio Lucio Vivaldi (1678-1741), one of the greatest Baroque composers that Italy had ever produced. He was a composer, a violinist, a priest and a teacher who was famous for composing the highly popular 'The Four Seasons' concertos played on the violin, a classic piece that is currently played the most among his compositions. He left a decisive mark on the form of the concerto and the style of late Baroque instrumental music. His concertos and arias had a great influence on the compositions made by John Sebastian Bach.

①**Bach:** Johann Sebastian Bach (1685-1750) , a German composer and an outstanding organist, violinist, harpsichordist and musician of the Baroque period. He was considered "the father of all modern western music" and became its "never to be surpassed musical peak". He is known for instrumental compositions such as the *Brandenburg Concertos* and the *Goldberg Variantions*, and vocal music such as the *St Matthew Passion* and *the Mass in B minor*.

当我瞥向他时,他的脸
就是一幅全神贯注的画面
完全沉浸在音乐里的他
那份专注并未因我而分散

①**维瓦尔第**:安东尼奥·卢奇奥·维瓦尔第(1678—1741),意大利巴洛克时期最著名的作曲家之一。他还是小提琴演奏家、神父、老师。其作品数量颇丰,大协奏曲《四季》是他最著名的作品之一,其作品对巴赫的创作有重要影响。

②**巴赫**:约翰·塞巴斯蒂安·巴赫(1685—1750),巴洛克时期的德国作曲家,杰出的管风琴、小提琴、大键琴演奏家。被誉为"近代音乐之父""不可超越的大师"。代表作品有《勃兰登堡协奏曲》《哥德堡变奏曲》《马太受难曲》《b小调弥撒曲》等。

HE

She said she liked classical music.
I implied I was keen on it too.
Though I don't often go to a concert,
It wasn't entirely untrue.

I looked for a suitable concert
And here we are, on our first date.
The traffic was dreadful this evening
And I arrived ten minutes late.

So we haven't had much time for talking
And I'm a bit nervous. I see
She is totally lost in the music
And quite undistracted by me.

In that dress she is very attractive—
The neckline can't fail to intrigue.
I mustn't appear too besotted.
Perhaps she is out of my league.

Where are we? I glance at the programme
But I've put my glasses away.

他

她说她喜欢古典音乐
我暗示她我也喜欢
虽然我不常去音乐会
可事实确实如此

这不,在我们的第一次约会
我就找了一个合适的音乐会
今晚的交通糟糕透顶
我竟迟了十分钟

没有太多的时间交谈
我有点惴惴不安
她完全沉浸在音乐里
那份专注并未因我而分散

身着漂亮裙子的她很是迷人
仅那领口就令人销魂
我一定不能表现得太痴迷
也许我不符合她的标准

节目进行到哪儿啦?想看下节目单
可眼镜没带来

I'd better start paying attention

Or else I'll have nothing to say.

我还是认真聆听吧
否则以什么做谈资

Football

A most delightful programme
Goes out on Saturday
When football fans ring Radio 5,
All keen to have their say.

Caller after caller
Whose team is doing badly
Will tell us what the problem is,
More angrily than sadly.

There are two explanations
For failure, as a rule:
The referee's a villain or
The manager's a fool.

The Radio 5 presenter
Is rational and calm,
Defending refs against the men
Who want to do them harm,

Who want them to be punished

足 球

周六，当一帮球迷
给BBC第五台致电
精彩的节目就开始上演
他们都渴望发表自己的观点

当球迷们支持的队伍表现不佳
电话便应接不暇
告诉我们出了什么差错
生气胜过难过

对于失利，按照惯例
有两种解释：
要么裁判是无赖
要么主教练是蠢货

第五电台的播音员
冷静沉着
为了不使裁判员受到伤害
极力辩解着

球迷们希望裁判

For their defective vision—

Dismissed, disgraced and disembowelled

For every bad decision.

The righteous rage! The passion!

I'm not a football fan

But this is first-rate comedy.

I listen when I can.

因视觉误差被惩处
被开除、受辱、被开膛
为那每一个糟糕的判罚遭殃

这义愤！这激情！
我不是足球迷
但这是一流的喜剧
有机会我就聆听

Lissadell

Last year we went to **Lissadell**[①].
The sun shone over **Sligo Bay**[②]
And life was good and all was well.

The bear, the books, the dinner-bell,
An air of dignified decay.
Last year we went to Lissadell.

This year the owners had to sell –
It calls to mind a Chekhov play[③].
Once life was good and all was well.

The house is now an empty shell,
The contents auctioned, shipped away.
Last year we went to Lissadell

And found it magical. 'We fell
In love with it', we sometimes say
When life is good and all is well.

The light of evening. A gazelle[④].

丽萨德尔庄园*

去年我们去了丽萨德尔庄园①
太阳照在斯莱戈湾②
岁月静好,一切安然

毛绒熊、书籍、就餐铃
处处显露出家道的中落
去年我们去了丽萨德尔庄园

今年庄园被迫出售——
我不由想起契诃夫的戏剧《樱桃园》③
昔日的樱桃园岁月静好,一切安然

现在的庄园只剩一个空壳
里面的物品被拍卖、运走
去年我们去了丽萨德尔庄园

感受到它独有的魅力,我们不由会说
"我们爱上它了"
只觉着岁月静好,一切安然

"夜晚的光亮,一只羚羊"④

---

* 请参阅附录P206。

It seemed unchanged since Yeats's day.

Last year we went to Lissadell.

And life was good and all was well.

①**Lissadell:** It is the name of the demesne which is attached to Lissadell House, a neo-classical Greek revivalist style country house, located in County Sligo, Ireland, built between 1830 and 1835. Lissadell is famous as the childhood home of Irish revolutionary Constance Markievicz, her sister the poet of distinction and an active suffragist Eva Gore-Booth and her brother Josslyn Gore-Booth. The great poet W. B. Yeats was friendly with the Gore Booth sisters and stayed at Lissadell in 1892 and 1893. He immortalised Lissadell and the Gore Booth sisters in his poetry *In Memory of Eva Gore-Booth and Con Markiewicz.*

②**Sligo Bay:** A natural ocean bay in County Sligo, Republic of Ireland.

③**Chekhov play:** *The Cherry Orchard* is the last play by Russian writer Anton Chekhov written in 1903. The play concerns the aristocratic Russian landowners (Ranevskaya and her brother Gayev) whose estate (which includes a large and well-known cherry orchard) is auctioned to pay off the family's debts.

④**The light of evening. A gazelle:** They are borrowed from *In Memory of Eva Gore-Booth and Con Markiewicz* by John Butler Yeats.

那里从叶芝的时代起就一直那样
去年我们去了丽萨德尔庄园
岁月静好，一切安然

①**丽萨德尔庄园**：这幢位于爱尔兰斯莱戈镇的乡村豪宅建于1830至1835年，是一幢新古典主义的建筑。该庄园是爱尔兰女革命家康斯坦斯·马凯维奇和其作为一个杰出的诗人和女权运动的积极分子的妹妹埃娃·高尔布斯及其兄弟们童年时的住所。爱尔兰诗人叶芝和姐妹俩过从甚密，曾于1892和1893在此居住。他的诗歌《怀念埃娃·高尔布斯和康·马凯维奇》使昔日的豪宅和姐妹俩永载史册。
②**斯莱戈湾**：位于爱尔兰共和国斯莱戈镇的一个天然海湾。
③**《樱桃园》**：俄国作家契诃夫于1903年创作的最后一部戏剧。该剧讲述俄国贵族加耶夫、郎涅夫斯卡雅兄妹被迫出卖祖传的樱桃园。
④**夜晚的光亮，一只羚羊**：该诗行引自爱尔兰诗人叶芝的诗歌 《怀念埃娃·高尔布斯和康·马凯维奇》（*In Memory of Eva Gore-Booth and Con Markiewicz*）的诗行。（这里的羚羊指美丽的姑娘Eva Gore-Booth，诗人叶芝把身着日本和服的美丽的姑娘Eva Gore-Booth描述为一只羚羊，暗喻她的激进思想与豪华的丽萨德尔庄园格格不入。）

At Steep[1]

We stumble down the sloping path
Clutching at trunks and branches, then
A few more steps, another tree,
Until at last we see the stone.

'That must be it.' There is no sign
On road or path to say it's there
But walkers pass this way and learn
Your name and find out who you were,

And pilgrims clutching leaflets come
From time to time, walk half a mile
To sit by your memorial
And keep you company awhile.

No. You're beyond all company.
Numbers and words inscribed on stone
Are all that's left of you where once
You felt the sun, the blessed rain.

Numbers and words inscribed on stone.

在斯蒂普[①]

我们踉跄在陡峭的山路上
抱住一些树干，攫住一些枝蔓，继而
再向前几步，抓住另一棵树
直到看见那石碑

"那一定就是"
无论是大路上还是小径旁，都没有明确的路牌
但途经那里的路人得知了你的名字
发现了你的传奇

朝圣者们手持小册子
时不时来此觐见
步行半英里，坐在纪念碑旁
陪你半晌

不。谁也无法陪你
刻在石碑上的数字和文字
是你留下的唯一。你曾在这里
感受过阳光和细雨

数字和文字刻在石碑上

You're dead and gone and speaking still.

Your spirit lives; it brought us here.

You cannot know, and never will.

①Edward Thomas lived at Steep in Hampshire. There is a memorial to him on a hillside outside the village.

你死了,走了,却依然在叙说
你的精神活着。我们为此觐见此地
你不知道,永不知道

①**斯蒂普**:爱德华·托马斯(参阅P140)曾在英国汉普郡的斯蒂普居住过,如今在村外的山坡上竖立着他的纪念碑。

Probably

If I'm not sure, I can't say yes.
You need an answer by today.
Probably. Unless. Unless

I've freaked from all the strain and stress,
They've come and carted me away.
If I'm not sure, I can't say yes.

If I'm alive, at this address,
I'll try to do it. I can say
Probably. Unless. Unless

I'm down with flu or in some mess
So dire that I can't work or play.
If I'm not sure, I can't say yes.

I cannot guarantee success.
I'll blow it, forfeiting the pay,
Probably. Unless. Unless

也 许*

没有把握，我无法给你承诺
今天你就要一个明确的结果
也许，除非，除非

紧张和压力已使我崩溃
把我送往精神病医院的人们挟持了我
没有把握，我无法给你承诺

只要还在此地活着
我尽力而为。我会说
也许，除非，除非

流感使我卧床不起，加之别的困境
使我不能娱乐，也无法工作
没有把握，我无法给你承诺

我不能保证成功
我会把一切搞砸，丢了报酬
也许，除非，除非

---

* 请参阅附录P207。

I ask for help in my distress.

Does someone hear me when I pray?

If I'm not sure, I can't say yes.

Probably. Unless. Unless

困苦中的我请求帮助
有人听到我的祈祷了吗?
没有把握,我不能给你承诺
也许,除非,除非

A Reading

Everybody in this room is bored.
The poems drag, the voice and gestures irk.
He can't be interrupted or ignored.

Poor fools, we came here of our own accord,
And some of us have paid to hear this jerk.
Everybody in this room is bored.

The silent cry goes up, 'How long, O Lord?'
But nobody will scream or go berserk.
He won't be interrupted or ignored.

Or hit by eggs, or savaged by a horde
Of desperate people maddened by his work.
Everybody in this room is bored,

Except the poet. We are his reward,
Pretending to indulge his every quirk.
He won't be interrupted or ignored.

At last it's over. How we all applaud!

一场朗诵会

室内的每个人都觉着乏味至极
拖泥带水的诗歌、令人厌倦的声音和手势
你不能打断他,也不能忽视他

我们都是自愿来的,真是可怜的傻子。
一些人还是买票来听的
室内的每个人都觉得乏味至极

悄然的呐喊"上帝啊,怎么这么长?"
但无人尖叫,无人狂躁
不能打断他,也不能忽视他

不能用鸡蛋砸他,更不能让一帮人围攻他
绝望的人们要被他的作品折磨疯了
室内的每个人都觉得乏味至极

除了诗人本人。给他的酬劳就是假装
陶醉于他的每一个癖好
不能打断他,也不能忽视他

终于结束了。全场热烈地鼓掌

The poet thanks us with a modest smirk.

Everybody in the room bored.

He wasn't interrupted or ignored.

诗人向我们致谢，露出一丝得意
室内的每个人都觉得乏味至极
不能打断他，也不能忽视他

Serious Concerns

Write to amuse? What appalling suggestion!

I write to make people anxious and miserable and to worsen their indigestion.

关　切

创作是为了逗乐？这建议令人惊愕！
我创作为了使一些人焦虑、难过，让其消化道堵塞。

Sonnet

(inspired by Sonnet 22)

My glass can't quite persuade me I am old –
In that respect my ageing eyes are kind –
But when I see a photograph, I'm told
The dismal truth: I've left my youth behind.
And when I try to get up from a chair
My knees remind me they are past their best.
The burden they have carried everywhere
Is heavier now. No wonder they protest.
Arthritic fingers, problematic neck,
Sometimes causing mild to moderate pain,
Could well persuade me I'm an ancient wreck
But here's what helps me to feel young again:
  My love, who fell for me so long ago,
  Still loves me just as much, and tells me so.

十四行诗（受莎士比亚十四行诗No.22的启发而作）

镜子并未使我意识到容颜已老——

这么说来，我的老花眼还挺仁慈的——

但我看到的一张照片向我袒露了

一个严酷的事实：青春早已远离了我

当我从椅子上起身

膝盖提醒我它们已不如往日那般灵活

曾载着我东奔西跑的它们

现在有点不堪重荷

患有关节炎的手指和有颈椎病的颈脖

时不时会痛，饱受各种疼痛的折磨

这一切终让我意识到——我这台设备老化了

但仍有一样又让我感受到了青春的气息

我的爱人，是你！爱了我许多年的你

依然像以前那样爱着我，依然表白着

附 录

感谢Martin和Wendy在我翻译过程中通过邮件为我答疑解惑。本书中的注解皆源自他们邮件里的答案或在邮件的启示下查阅的资料。为了方便喜欢英语诗歌的读者更好地欣赏英语原文，在此特附几封Martin和Wendy的邮件。

On a Train

From Maritn

Q4: Do "winter trees" here mean the trees in winter generally, or they are a special kind of tree?

I think this refers to the aspect of deciduous trees in a northern temperate winter.

I.e. no leaves. Perhaps also to the evergreen trees which stand out more.

But only the poet will know what was in her mind.

From Wendy

Dear Yan,

Martin Bishop is right. They were deciduous trees with no leaves in winter.

Please note that the last line should read

"Every car park a shining mosaic". (you left out "a").

I'll be happy to answer any questions you have in future.

Best wishes,

Wendy

Valentine

From Martin:

Q1: And I'm afraid it's you: Does the author mean "I think it's you that I want to marry(or choose to be a Valentine)" or "It is you that I worry about"?

Over apologetic English
http://www.bbcamerica.com/shows//blog/2013/02/gosh-sorry-overapologetic-brits-in-america

"For many British people, apologizing is a default reaction to life's little irritants. If someone barges into you, treads on your toes or spills your drink, it is considered quite normal for the victim to mutter 'sorry'. This is clearly illogical, but for many British people it is an ingrained response."

She is not sorry at all but has chosen him/her as an object of sexual desire.

Q2. Whatever you've got lined up: Does it mean I do not care about whomever you have been after?

Whatever you intend to do I have chosen you and repeats the "afraid" when not in the least regretful.

Wendy must be very English as well as christian and moral.

From Wendy
Dear Yan,

Yes, Martin is right. She has chosen him. She says "I'm afraid it's you" because he might not want to be chosen. But tough luck, he has been. So, yes, it's a kind of apology. There is no resigned dread.

"Whatever you've got lined up" means whatever you intend to do, as Martin says.

You might be interested to know that my heart changed its mind not long after I wrote the poem—this is not about the man I married.
Best wishes,
Wendy

Being Boring
Dear Yan,

When we call someone a vegetable we mean they are inactive and uninteresting. A cabbage is considered an especially boring vegetable. So, what I am saying is "I am happy to be a cabbage." "My vegetable spirits are soaring" means I am very happy to be a vegetable. This should not be taken too seriously, of course.

If a person watches too much television, we call them a couch potato.

I hope that helps.

Best wishes,

Wendy

Proverbial Ballade

Puzzle Dear Yan,

Don't worry about occupying my time. I appreciate the trouble you are taking with these translations.

My poem "Proverbial Ballade" is made up of joke proverbs—that is, lines that sound as though they might be proverbs although they are not.

A wild rose has no employees. Employees: people who are employed. Obviously a flower doesn't employ anybody. But it sounds like a proverb. Well, that's the idea.

You can't shave with a tiddlywink. Tiddlywinks is a children's game played with plastic counters. Again, this is too obvious to be worth saying but it sounds as if it could be a proverb.

Does this make sense, Yan? If not, please write again.

Best wishes,

Wendy

Tich Miller

From Martin

Q1: Could I translate larger just directly into Chinese (larger /bigger)?

Yes, but the size difference would be defined by a table such as

http://www.dancesport.uk.com/shoes/conchart.htm

Q2 : What does the underlined part mean?

We avoided one another's eyes,

stooping, perhaps, to re-tie a shoelace,

<u>*or affecting interest in the flight*</u>

They made it look as though they were interested in the flight of a bird passing by

'Have Tubby!' 'No, no, have Tich!'

http://www.babble.com/kid/why-kids-mean-aggressive/

tubby = fatty; tich = tiny

Martin

From Wendy

Hello Yan,

Yes Tich means little. It is a nickname often given to people who are small. Little is fine with me. Or perhaps there is an affectionate name Chinese people give to someone small.

Are you OK with Tubby, later on in the poem? That means fat. Sometimes fat children get called "Fatty". That is unkind, rather than affectionate. I hope there's a suitable Chinese word for it.

It's very hot here today. We grumble about the British weather. Then, when we get some sunshine, we all complain that we're too hot.

All good wishes,

Wendy

After the Lunch

Hello Yanping.

Here are answers to your questions. The speaker of the poem has just had lunch with someone and realises, as she crosses Waterloo Bridge, that she has fallen in love with him. She argues with herself, asking if she is really in love or if it is just the effect of his charm and the wine she has been drinking.

There is an argument between the head and the heart. "The head" is the sensible, rational part of her. "The heart" represents her emotions. Before she is halfway across Waterloo Bridge she has stopped arguing with herself and admitted that she has fallen in love.

I hope this helps.

Thanks very much for the kind things you say about my work.

Best wishes,

Wendy

On Finding an Old Photograph / Another Valentine's Day

Dear Yan,

Here are answer to your other two questions.

"On Finding an Old Photograph". Yes, the burden is mine. They say everyone feels guilty when a parent dies. You think of all the times you could have done more to make them happy. The photograph reminds me that my father was alive for a long time before I was born. I wasn't responsible for his life. He was 59 years old when I was born.

"Another Valentine". St Valentine's Day on 14th February is traditionally a time for romance. People send cards saying "Will you be my valentine?" Often these cards are anonymous. Men buy flowers, usually red roses, for their partners and couples go out for romantic dinners. The result is that red roses and restaurants are very expensive on that day, so sensible people go out to dinner some other time. My husband always buys me one red rose and we give each other a card and a present.

Best wishes,

Wendy

From Strugnell's Rubáiyát

Dear Yan,

I'm glad you and your husband like that stanza.

In Strugnells Rubaiyat my invented poet, Jason Strugnell, has decided to update The Rubaiyat of Omar kyayyam, introducing contemporary language. It's terible, of course, but it's meant to be funny. You've probably worked that out already. The version of the Rubaiyat that English people read is the 19th century translation by Edward Fitzgerald.

Stanza 26 begins "Oh, come with old Khayam". So Strugnell begins his "Oh, come with Strugnell".

Fitzgerald: "and leave the Wise/ to talk", Strugnell. "Argument's no Tonic"—that is, sitting around arguing doesn't make you feel any better.

Fitzgerald: "one thing is certain, that Life flies". Strugnell "One thing's certain: Life flies supersonic".

Fitzgerald: "One thing is certain, and the Rest is Lies" Strugnell: "One thing's certain, Man's evasion chronic". That is, man's reluctance to face the truth is like a chronic illness.

Fitzgerald. "The Flower that once has blown for ever dies". Strugnell "The flower that's blown can never be bionic". There were films called The Bionic Man and The Bionic Woman. The idea was that badly injured people could be given artificial body parts. This made them superheroes.

Strugnell is saying there is nothing that can be done to revive a flower once its petals have blown away.

I've probably explained some things that didn't need explaining but l hope this helps.

Best wishes,

Wendy

From Strugnell's Sonnets(For D.M.Thomas) (V)

Dear Yan,

No you won't find any information because I invented the song and the group. This was in the punk-rock era.

I'm glad I don't have to figure out how to translate them into Chinese.

Best wishes

Wendy

Sent from my iPhone

Lissadell

Dear Wendy,

Sorry, I have some questions which only you can answer.

Q1: What's the real meaning of the Bear in the lines? Martin gives me several explanations, which makes me more confused.

Q2: Whats the connection between "It calls to mind a Chekhov play." and "Once life was good and all was well." The later has almost been regarded by me as a refrain, yet you add "Once" here.

Without "once" such as the last line of the first stanza, you use the past tense. With "Once" here, the tense here is still past tense. So, please enlighten me! Many many thanks!

Sweet regards,

Yan

Dear Yan,

There was a stuffed bear in the house.

The Chekhov play it calls to mind is *The Cherry Orchard*. The owners have to sell their house. Once (before that) they had a good life.

The owners of Lissadell had to sell their house shortly after we visited it. Once (before that) they too had a good life.

Do you understand now? If not, please write again.

All good wishes,

Wendy

Probably

I've freaked from all the strain and sress,
They've come and carted me away.
If I'm not sure, I can't say yes.

Q1: Does "They" refer to the strain and stress in the above line?

There is no more questions to trouble you for the time being!

Thank you very much.

Best wishes,

Yours

Yan

Dear Yan:

Answer to your questions:

In the line "They've come and carted me away", "they" are the people who would take a mentally ill person to hospital.

Hope that's clear.

Best wishes,

Wendy

译后记

在英国剑桥大学英语系一年的访学经历是我一生的财富。在剑桥大学邂逅了牛津大学《生物信息简报》(*Briefings in Bioinformatics*)的主编Martin John Bishop教授是我访学期间的一大收获。正是他一直以来的无私帮助才使我在继《托马斯·胡德诗选》《英语美文》之后有了《又见情人节:温迪·蔻普诗选》。我们之间的邮件串起来可以写一本与《查令十字街84号》相媲美的书。

最早读到温迪的诗是在英国剑桥大学英语系,那是2013年的情人节。英语系图书馆馆长Libby Tilley为了庆祝情人节,不仅在图书馆内摆上了红红的玫瑰花,还在图书馆的墙壁、门、廊柱等处贴上了许多红纸剪成的大的爱心,每个红色爱心中部贴有一首英美情诗。第一次感受到这么浪漫、温馨的情人节,我无比欣喜地尽情欣赏着一首首被爱心捧着的情诗。当我读到温迪的《午饭后》(*After the Lunch*)时,我困惑:这是情诗吗?我又读了第二遍、第三遍,情感偏内敛的我体悟到了诗中矜持的女主角内心那份欲罢不能的炽热情愫。我喜欢上了这首情诗。因为这首诗,我开始了解诗作者温迪,了解到她是英国颇受欢迎的当代女诗人。

感谢诗人温迪,她不仅通过邮件解答了该诗选翻译、出版过程中遇到的各种问题(文本理解问题、版权问题),在我拜访她时，还亲自驾车到火车站接送我。能和她及其丈夫在他们鲜花盛开的后花园里一起度过那个阳光明媚的下午，我深感荣幸。感念温迪夫妇的友好款待和签名赠书。

翻译温迪诗作时，我像以往一样，把译文分享给一些朋友、学生，请他们提宝贵意见。感谢昔日同窗田海斌总是欣然接受读初稿这个艰巨任务，并提出合理的建议，感谢西安市育才中学校长于颉老师的专业点评，感谢昔日的研究生、现在的同行陈韵姿、林静及研究生刘慧敏，本科生刘浩宇等的鼎力相助，感谢诸位的辛苦付出。

相对于诸多"不知所云"的现代诗，温迪的诗"言之有物""言之有理""言之有情"。我竭尽全力把她的佳作译成汉语，以飨国内读者，但我也深知自己才疏学浅，不妥之处在所难免。常言说，"有最佳的作品，没有最佳的译作"，请各位读者和同仁不吝赐教，使英国女诗人温迪诗歌的译文能够日臻完美。